Compact
Kansas
BIRDS

Ted T. Cable, Scott Seltman,
Krista Kagume & Gregory Kennedy

LONE PINE

Lone Pine Publishing International

© 2007 by Lone Pine Publishing International Inc.
First printed in 2007   10 9 8 7 6 5 4 3 2 1
Printed in China

The Distributor: Lone Pine Publishing
1808 B Street NW, Suite 140
Auburn, WA, USA 98001

Website: www.lonepinepublishing.com

Library and Archives Canada Cataloguing in Publication

Compact guide to Kansas birds / Ted T. Cable ... [et al.].

Includes bibliographical references and index.
ISBN 978-976-8200-25-9

1. Birds--Kansas--Identification. I. Cable, Ted T.

QL684.K2C332 2007   598'.09781   C2006-906334-6

Illustrations: Gary Ross, Ted Nordhagen, Ewa Pluciennik
Cover Illustration: Red-winged Blackbird by Ted Nordhagen
Egg Photography: Alan Bibby, Gary Whyte
Scanning and Digital Film: Elite Lithographers Co.

We wish to thank the Royal Alberta Museum for providing access to their egg collections.

PC: P13

Contents

4 Reference Guide

Snow Goose
size 32 in • p. 20

Canada Goose
size 42 in • p. 22

Wood Duck
size 17 in • p. 24

Gadwall
size 20 in • p. 26

Mallard
size 24 in • p. 28

Blue-winged Teal
size 15 in • p. 30

Lesser Scaup
size 16 in • p. 32

Common Goldeneye
size 18 in • p. 34

Common Merganser
size 25 in • p. 36

Ring-necked Pheasant
size 34 in • p. 38

Greater Prairie-Chicken
size 17 in • p. 40

Wild Turkey
size 39 in • p. 42

Northern Bobwhite
size 10 in • p. 44

Pied-billed Grebe
size 13 in • p. 46

American White Pelican
size 63 in • p. 48

Double-crested Cormorant
size 29 in • p. 50

Great Blue Heron
size 51 in • p. 52

Great Egret
size 39 in • p. 54

Black-crowned Night-Heron
size 24 in • p. 56

Turkey Vulture
size 28 in • p. 58

Mississippi Kite
size 14 in • p. 60

Bald Eagle
size 36 in • p. 62

Northern Harrier
size 20 in • p. 64

Cooper's Hawk
size 17 in • p. 66

Swainson's Hawk
size 21 in • p. 68

Red-tailed Hawk
size 21 in • p. 70

Rough-legged Hawk
size 22 in • p. 72

American Kestrel
size 8 in • p. 74

American Coot
size 15 in • p. 76

Killdeer
size 10 in • p. 78

Spotted Sandpiper
size 8 in • p. 80

Lesser Yellowlegs
size 11 in • p. 82

Baird's Sandpiper
size 7 in • p. 84

Franklin's Gull
size 14 in • p. 86

Ring-billed Gull
size 19 in • p. 88

Forster's Tern
size 15 in • p. 90

Rock Pigeon
size 13 in • p. 92

Eurasian Collared-Dove
size 12 in • p. 94

Mourning Dove
size 12 in • p. 96

Eastern Screech-Owl
size 9 in • p. 98

Great Horned Owl
size 22 in • p. 100

Barred Owl
size 20 in • p. 102

Common Nighthawk
size 9 in • p. 104

Chimney Swift
size 5 in • p. 106

Ruby-throated Hummingbird
size 4 in • p. 108

Belted Kingfisher
size 13 in • p. 110

Red-headed Woodpecker
size 9 in • p. 112

Red-bellied Woodpecker
size 9 in • p. 114

Downy Woodpecker
size 7 in • p. 116

Northern Flicker
size 13 in • p. 118

Least Flycatcher
size 5 in • p. 120

Eastern Phoebe
size 7 in • p. 122

Great Crested Flycatcher
size 8 in • p. 124

Western Kingbird
size 9 in • p. 126

Eastern Kingbird
size 8 in • p. 128

Loggerhead Shrike
size 9 in • p. 130

Warbling Vireo
size 5 in • p. 132

Blue Jay
size 12 in • p. 134

Black-billed Magpie
size 18 in • p. 136

American Crow
size 18 in • p. 138

Horned Lark
size 7 in • p. 140

Purple Martin
size 8 in • p. 142

Tree Swallow
size 5 in • p. 144

Cliff Swallow
size 5 in • p. 146

Barn Swallow
size 7 in • p. 148

Black-capped Chickadee
size 5 in • p. 150

Tufted Titmouse
size 6 in • p. 152

White-breasted Nuthatch
size 6 in • p. 154

Carolina Wren
size 5 in • p. 156

House Wren
size 5 in • p. 158

Golden-crowned Kinglet
size 4 in • p. 160

Eastern Bluebird
size 7 in • p. 162

KINGLETS & THRUSHES

American Robin
size 10 in • p. 164

Gray Catbird
size 9 in • p. 166

Northern Mockingbird
size 10 in • p. 168

MIMICS, STARLINGS & WAXWINGS

Brown Thrasher
size 11 in • p. 170

European Starling
size 8 in • p. 172

Cedar Waxwing
size 7 in • p. 174

WOOD-WARBLERS & TANAGERS

Orange-crowned Warbler
size 5 in • p. 176

Yellow Warbler
size 5 in • p. 178

Yellow-rumped Warbler
size 5 in • p. 180

Common Yellowthroat
size 5 in • p. 182

Summer Tanager
size 7 in • p. 184

Spotted Towhee
size 8 in • p. 186

SPARROWS & ALLIES

American Tree Sparrow
size 6 in • p. 188

Chipping Sparrow
size 6 in • p. 190

Grasshopper Sparrow
size 5 in • p. 192

Song Sparrow
size 6 in • p. 194

Harris's Sparrow
size 7 in • p. 196

White-crowned Sparrow
size 6 in • p. 198

Dark-eyed Junco
size 7 in • p. 200

Longspur Lapland
size 6 in • p. 202

Northern Cardinal
size 8 in • p. 204

Indigo Bunting
size 5 in • p. 206

Painted Bunting
size 5 in • p. 208

Dickcissel
size 6 in • p. 210

SPARROWS & ALLIES

Red-winged Blackbird
size 8 in • p. 212

Western Meadowlark
size 9 in • p. 214

Common Grackle
size 12 in • p. 216

BLACKBIRDS & ALLIES

Brown-headed Cowbird
size 8 in • p. 218

Oriole Baltimore
size 8 in • p. 220

House Finch
size 6 in • p. 222

Pine Siskin
size 5 in • p. 224

American Goldfinch
size 5 in • p. 226

House Sparrow
size 6 in • p. 228

FINCHLIKE BIRDS

Introduction

If you have ever admired a songbird's pleasant notes, been fascinated by a soaring hawk or wondered how woodpeckers keep sawdust out of their nostrils, this book is for you. There is so much to discover about birds and their surroundings that birding is becoming one of the fastest-growing hobbies on the planet. Many people find it relaxing, while others enjoy its outdoor appeal. Some people see it as a way to reconnect with nature, an opportunity to socialize with like-minded people or a way to monitor the environment.

Northern Harrier

Whether you are just beginning to take an interest in birds or can already identify many species, there is always more to learn. We've highlighted both the remarkable traits and the more typical behaviors displayed by some of our most abundant or noteworthy birds. A few live in specialized habitats, but most are common species that you have a good chance of encountering on most outings or in your backyard.

BIRDING IN KANSAS

We are truly blessed by the geographical and biological diversity of Kansas. In addition to supporting a wide range of breeding birds and year-round residents, our state hosts a large number of spring and fall migrants that move through our area on the way to their breeding and wintering grounds. In all, 469 bird species have been seen and recorded in Kansas.

Identifying birds in action and under varying conditions involves skill, timing and luck. The more you know about a bird—its range, preferred habitat, food preferences and hours of activity—the better your chances will be of seeing it. Generally, spring and fall are the busiest birding seasons because the temperatures are moderate and many species of birds are migrating. In spring, male songbirds tend to acquire their brightest plumage and begin to belt out their unique songs in hopes of attracting a mate, making them easier to spot. Throughout the year, birds are typically most active in the early morning hours, except perhaps in winter when birds often delay their search for food until midday.

Western Kingbird

Finding birds requires knowledge of their "habitat", a word that describes the place where they normally live. Some birds prefer lakes, some are found in cattail marshes, others are in grasslands while others live only in forests. Habitats are like neighborhoods. If you can recognize the neighborhoods where your friends and families live, you already possess the skills necessary to learn the preferred habitats of specific types of birds. Some birds never leave their normal habitats except in migration.

Learning to recognize birds by their songs and calls can greatly enhance your birding experience and will often simplify the identification of birds in the field. Numerous tapes and CDs are available to help learn bird songs. Beginner and veteran birders alike often find it useful to carry a compact personal stereo with headphones to assist in matching birds with their calls. Before the age of portable sound, birders often made up catchy mnemonic phrases to help them describe and remember various calls. We have included a few of these old-fashioned renderings in the species accounts that follow. Some of these often humorous phrases work better than others; individual birds will sometimes alter their songs by adding or deleting syllables, and within most species there is geographic variation in the way entire populations sing.

Kansas has a long tradition of friendly, recreational birding. In general, birders are willing to help beginners, share their knowledge and involve novices in their projects. Christmas bird counts, breeding bird surveys, nest box programs, migration monitoring, and birding lectures and workshops provide a chance for birdwatchers of all levels to interact and share the splendor of birds. A birding listserv and website provides up-to-date information on the sightings of rarities, which are often easier to relocate than you might think. For more information or to participate in these projects, contact the following organizations:

Kansas Ornithological Society
www.ksbirds.org

Audubon of Kansas
210 Southwind Place
Manhattan, KS 66503
Phone: 785-537-4385
www.audubonofkansas.org

Great Plains Nature Center
6232 E. 29 St. North
Wichita, KS 67220-2200
Phone: 316-683-5499
www.gpnc.org

BIRD LISTING

Many birders keep lists of the birds they have seen in their backyards or while visiting a favorite hotspot. These lists may include birds seen on just one day or perhaps all the species seen at a given place in a lifetime. It is up to you to decide what kind of list—systematic or casual—you will keep or whether you will keep any lists at all. There are, however, several good reasons to keep track of the things that you see. Over time, the checklists you fill in will become valuable souvenirs of the places you have visited. They will also allow you to compare arrival and last departure dates of various seasonal visitors that may visit your home, such as hummingbirds. Plus the records a birder keeps may often prove very valuable to researchers in the study of bird populations or those attempting to preserve wild-life habitat.

Barred Owl

BIRD FEEDING

People everywhere love to feed birds, and by choosing the right kind of food and style of feeder, you will likely attract many kinds of birds to your own backyard. In Kansas, large numbers of sparrows and other seed-eating birds will visit a feeder in winter. Keep your feeder stocked through

Common Yellowthroat

late spring, because birds have a hard time finding food before the flowers bloom, seeds develop and insects hatch. Contrary to popular belief, birds do not become dependent on feeders, nor do they subsequently forget to forage naturally. Be sure to clean your feeder and the surrounding area regularly to prevent the spread of disease.

Landscaping your property with native plants is another way of providing natural food for birds. Flocks of waxwings have a keen eye for redcedar berries and crab apples, whereas hummingbirds enjoy columbine, salvia or trumpet vine flowers. The cumulative effects of "naturescaping" urban yards can be a significant step toward habitat conservation. Many good books and websites about attracting wildlife to your backyard are available.

Northern Bobwhite

NEST BOXES
Another popular way to attract birds is to put up nest boxes, especially for House Wrens, Eastern Bluebirds, and Purple Martins. Larger nest boxes can attract kestrels, owls and cavity-nesting ducks like the Wood Duck.

Wood Duck

ABOUT THE SPECIES ACCOUNTS

This book gives detailed accounts of 105 species of birds that can be expected in Kansas on an annual basis. The order of the birds and their common and scientific names follow the American Ornithologists' Union's *Check-list of North American Birds* (7th edition, July 1998, and its supplements through 2006).

As well as showing the identifying features of the bird, each species account also attempts to bring the bird to life by describing its various character traits. One of the challenges of birding is that many species look different in spring and summer than they do in fall and winter. Many species have breeding and non-breeding plumages, and immature birds often look different from their parents. This book does not try to describe or illus-trate all the different plum-ages of a species; instead, it tries to focus on the forms that are most likely to be seen in our area.

Great Egret

ID: Large illustrations point out prominent field marks that will help you tell each bird apart. The descriptions favor easily understood language instead of technical terms.

Other ID: This section lists additional identifying features. Some of the most common anatomical features of birds are pointed out in the Glossary illustration (p. 231).

Size: The average length of the bird's body from bill to tail, as well as its wingspan, are given and are approximate measurements of the bird as it is seen in nature. The size is sometimes given as a range, because there is variation between individuals, or between males and females.

Voice: Many birds, especially songbirds, will often be easily heard and yet be very difficult to see. Memorable paraphrases of distinctive sounds will help you identify a species by ear.

Status: A general comment, such as "common," "uncommon" or "rare," is usually sufficient to describe the relative abundance of a species, but abundance can often vary due to migratory pulses and seasonal changes that will concentrate or disperse birds.

Habitat: The habitats listed describe where each species is most commonly found. Because of the freedom that flight gives them, birds can turn up in almost any type of habitat. However, they will usually be found in environments that provide the specific food, cover and nesting habitat they need to survive.

Painted Bunting

Similar Birds: Easily confused species are illustrated for each account. If you concentrate on the most relevant field marks, the subtle differences between species can be reduced to easily identifiable traits. Even experienced birders can mistake one species for another.

Nesting: In each species account, nest location and structure, clutch size, incubation period and parental duties are discussed. A photo of the bird's egg is also provided. Remember that birding ethics discourage the disturbance of active bird nests. If you disturb a nest, you may drive off the parents during a critical period or expose defenseless young to predators.

Range Maps: The range map for each species shows the overall range of the species in an average year. Most birds will confine their annual movements to this range, although each year some birds wander beyond their traditional boundaries. The maps show breeding, summer and winter ranges, as well as migratory pathways—areas of the region where birds may appear while en route to nesting or winter habitat. The representations of the pathways do not distinguish high-use migration corridors from areas that are seldom used.

Range Map Symbols

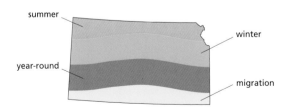

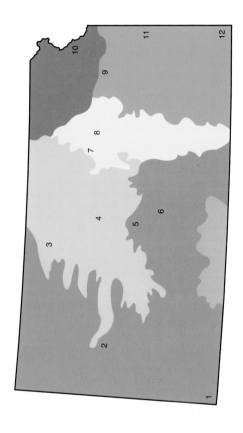

Ecoregions of Kansas

- High Plains
- Smoky Hills
- Arkansas Lowlands
- Red Hills
- Flint Hills
- Glaciated Region
- Osage Plains

TOP BIRDING SITES

From forested bluffs along the Missouri River to dry short-grass prairies dotted with cacti, our state can be separated into seven natural regions: High Plains, Smoky Hills, Arkansas Lowlands, Red Hills, Flint Hills, Glaciated Region and Osage Plains. Each region is composed of different habitats that support a wealth of wildlife.

There are many good birding areas throughout the state. The following areas have been selected to represent a broad range of bird communities and habitats, with an emphasis on accessibility.

1. Cimarron National Grasslands
2. Scott Lake State Park
3. Kirwin NWR
4. Wilson Reservoir
5. Cheyenne Bottoms WMA
6. Quivira NWR
7. Milford Reservoir
8. Konza Prairie
9. Clinton Reservoir
10. Ft Leavenworth
11. Marais des Cygnes NWR and WMA
12. Schermerhorn Park

NWR = National Wildlife Refuge
WMA = Wildlife Management Area

Snow Goose
Chen caerulescens

Snow Geese breed in the Arctic, some traveling as far as northeastern Siberia and crossing the Bering Strait twice a year. Their serrated bills are made for grazing on short arctic tundra and gripping the slippery roots of marsh plants. • Snow Geese can fly at speeds of up to 50 miles per hour. They are also strong walkers, and mothers have been known to lead their goslings up to 45 miles on foot in search of suitable habitat. • The Ross's Goose is nearly identical, but is much smaller with a smaller bill that lacks the black "grinning patch" seen on the Snow Goose.

Other ID: head often stained rusty red. *Blue morph:* uncommon; white head and upper neck; dark blue-gray body. *In flight:* black wing tips.
Size: L 30–33 in; W 4½–5 ft.
Voice: loud, nasal, *houk-houk* in flight, higher pitched and more constant than the Canada Goose's call.
Status: common to abundant migrant; winter resident in areas near open water.
Habitat: croplands, fields.

Similar Birds

Ross's Goose   Tundra Swan   Trumpeter Swan

black wing tips

dark "grin"
on bill

Nesting: does not nest in Kansas; nests in the Arctic; female builds the nest and lines it with grass, feathers and down; creamy white eggs are 3⅛ x 2 in; female incubates 4–7 eggs for 22–25 days.

Did You Know?

The Snow Goose has two color morphs, a white and a blue, which until 1983 were considered two different species.

Look For

Snow Geese fly in wavy, disorganized lines, whereas Canada Geese fly in a V-formation. Occasionally, mixed flocks form in migration.

Canada Goose
Branta canadensis

The Canada Goose was split into two species in 2004. The larger subspecies are known as Canada Geese, while the smaller subspecies have been renamed Cackling Geese. During migration look for Cackling Geese among flocks of Canada Geese.
• Rescuers who care for injured geese report that these birds readily adopt their human caregivers. However, wild geese can be aggressive, especially when defending young or competing for food. Hissing sounds and low, outstretched necks are signs that you should give these birds some space.

Other ID: dark brown upperparts; light brown underparts. *In flight:* flocks fly in V-formation.
Size: L 3–4 ft; W up to 6 ft.
Voice: loud, familiar *ah-honk.*
Status: common year-round resident, especially in parks and urban areas; numbers increase as migrants arrive; less common during severe winters.
Habitat: lakeshores, riverbanks, ponds, farmlands and city parks.

Similar Birds

Greater White-fronted Goose

Cackling Goose

"blue" morph of Snow Goose (immature)

long, black neck

white "chin strap"

short, black tail

white undertail coverts

Nesting: usually on the ground; female builds a nest of grass and mud, lined with down; white eggs are 3½ x 2¼ in; female incubates 3–8 eggs for 25–28 days; goslings hatch in May.

Did You Know?

Canada Geese mate for life and are devoted parents. Unlike most birds, the family stays together for nearly a year, which increases the survival rate of the young.

Look For

Geese graze on aquatic grasses and sprouts, but they can also be found eating the new growth of grasses on lawns and golf courses.

Wood Duck
Aix sponsa

As its name implies, the Wood Duck is a forest-dwelling duck, equipped with fairly sharp claws for perching on branches and nesting in tree cavities.

• Female Wood Ducks often return to the same nest site year after year, especially after successfully raising a brood. The young's chance of survival may increase at traditional nest sites, where the adults are familiar with potential threats. If Wood Ducks nest in a local park or farmyard, do not approach the nest, because fewer disturbances increase the young's chance of survival.

Other ID: *Male:* glossy, green head with some white streaks; white-spotted, purplish chestnut breast; dark back and hindquarters; long tail. *Female:* gray-brown upperparts; white belly.
Size: *L* 15–20 in; *W* 30 in.
Voice: *Male:* ascending *ter-wee-wee*. *Female:* squeaky *woo-e-e-k*.
Status: common summer resident and migrant in the eastern third of Kansas; uncommon in central and western Kansas; rare in winter in southeastern Kansas.
Habitat: swamps, ponds, marshes and lakeshores with wooded edges.

Similar Birds

Hooded Merganser

Look For

A male Wood Duck defending his mate from another suitor will often strike the interloper with an open wing when he gets too close.

raised head

white, teardrop-shaped eye patch

♀

crest is slicked back from crown

♀

♂

mottled brown breast is streaked with white

black and white shoulder slash

white chin and throat

Nesting: in a hollow, tree cavity or artificial nest box; usually near water; cavity is lined with down; white to buff eggs are 3⅛ x 1⅝ in; female incubates 9–14 eggs for 25–35 days.

Did You Know?

After hatching, ducklings must jump from their nest cavity to the ground, a distance of 20 feet or more. Like downy ping-pong balls, they bounce off the ground on landing, but they are seldom hurt.

Gadwall
Anas strepera

Gadwall numbers have recently reached record levels, with the North American population climbing to over 1.4 million breeding pairs in the 21st century. These medium-sized dabbling ducks are known for their lack of colorful plumage. Both sexes are grayish brown overall, with bold white wing patches. Males may be identified by their black rump and undertail coverts and females by their orange and brown bills. • Gadwalls feed on a variety of aquatic plants and invertebrates and are typically found in deeper water, farther from shore than other dabbling ducks.

Other ID: *Male:* dark above with a grayish brown head; dark eyes and bill; yellow legs; black breast patch and gray flanks.
Size: *L* 18–22 in; *W* 33 in.
Voice: both sexes quack like a Mallard.
Status: common migrant; uncommon summer and winter resident.
Habitat: freshwater lakes or ponds.

Similar Birds

American Wigeon

Mallard, female
(p. 28)

Northern Pintail

black upper- and undertail coverts

white speculum ♂

♀

brown bill with orange sides

♂

♀

gray or brown overall

white belly

Nesting: well-concealed nest is a grassy down-lined hollow placed in tall vegetation, sometimes far from water; creamy or pale green eggs are 2¼ x 1½ in; female incubates 8–11 eggs for 24–27 days.

Did You Know?

Gadwalls form monogamous pairs, and most females have found a mate by November, long before the start of the nesting season.

Look For

During winter, these ducks commonly feed in association with American Wigeons and American Coots.

Mallard
Anas platyrhynchos

Mallards can be seen
year-round, often in flocks
and always near open water.
After breeding, male ducks
lose their elaborate plumage, helping
them stay camouflaged during their flightless period.
In early fall, they molt back into breeding colors.
• Female ducks are mostly brown and often hard to
tell apart. Female American Black Ducks are darker
and lack the white edge to the blue speculum, female
Northern Shovelers have a big spoon-shaped bill,
and female Northern Pintails are more slender and
than female Mallards and lack the blue speculum.

Other ID: orange feet. *Male:* white "necklace"; black
tail feathers curl upward. *Female:* mottled brown overall.
In flight: dark blue speculum bordered by white.
Size: L 20–28 in; W 3 ft.
Voice: quacks; female is louder than male.
Status: abundant migrant and winter
resident near open water; uncommon
in summer.
Habitat: lakes, wetlands, rivers, city
parks, agricultural areas and sewage
lagoons.

Similar Birds

Northern Shoveler   American Black Duck   Mottled Duck

glossy, green head

yellow bill

orange bill
is spattered
with black

♂

♀

Nesting: female builds a grass nest on the
ground or under a bush; creamy, grayish or
greenish white eggs are 2¼ x 1⅝ in; female
incubates 7–10 eggs for 26–30 days.

Did You Know?

A nesting hen generates
enough body heat to
make the grasses around
her nest grow faster. She
uses the tall grasses to
further conceal her nest.

Look For

Mallards will freely hybridize
with domestic ducks and
American Black Ducks. The
resulting offspring are a confusing blend of both parental
types.

Blue-winged Teal
Anas discors

Small, speedy Blue-winged Teals are renowned for their aviation skills. They can be identified by their small size and the sharp twists and turns they execute in flight. • Blue-winged Teals and other dabbling ducks feed by tipping up their tails and dunking their heads underwater. Dabbling ducks have small feet situated near the center of their bodies. Other ducks, such as scaup, goldeneyes and Buffleheads, dive underwater to feed, propelled by large feet set farther back on their bodies. • Cinnamon Teals found in central and western Kansas have a wing pattern similar to that of the Blue-winged Teal.

Other ID: broad, flat bill. *Male:* white undertail coverts. *Female:* mottled brown overall.
Size: *L* 14–16 in; *W* 23 in.
Voice: *Male:* soft *keck-keck-keck*.
Female: soft quacks.
Status: common migrant and uncommon summer resident.
Habitat: shallow lake edges and wetlands; prefers areas with short but dense emergent vegetation.

Similar Birds

Green-winged Teal

Cinnamon Teal

white throat ♀

white crescent on face

blue-gray head

black-spotted breast and sides

♀

♂

Nesting: nests at Cheyenne Bottoms and other scattered locations in Kansas, but more commonly in the north-central U.S. and Canada; along a grassy shoreline or in a meadow; nest is built with grass and considerable amounts of down; whitish eggs are 1¾ x 1¼ in; female incubates 8–13 eggs for 23–27 days.

Did You Know?

Blue-winged Teals migrate farther than most ducks. They summer as far north as the Canadian tundra and overwinter mainly in Central and South America.

Look For

Blue-winged Teals are the first ducks to migrate in fall—look for them in early September. They are late to return in spring, with most arriving in mid- to late April.

Lesser Scaup
Aythya affinis

The male Scaup has a tricolored appearance like that of an Oreo cookie—black at both ends and white in the middle—that makes this widespread diving duck easy to recognize and remember. Two scaup species occur in Kansas and are most reliably separated by the amount of white in the wing, a field mark usually seen only in flight. The Lesser Scaup has a smaller white inner wing stripe that changes to dull gray on its primaries, whereas the Greater Scaup has a longer white stripe that extends into the primaries.

Other ID: small to medium-sized diving duck; gray-blue bill with black "nail" at tip; white wing stripe; highest point of head is above and behind eye. *Male:* white feathers of sides are dark tipped; grayish back; yellow eyes. *Female:* dark brown; white area encircles base of bill. *In flight:* white wing stripe.
Size: L 15–18 in; W 25 in.
Voice: generally silent in winter; alarm call is a deep *scaup. Male:* soft *whee-oooh* in courtship. *Female:* purring *kwah.*
Status: common migrant; rare in winter and summer.
Habitat: lakes, open marshes and along slow-moving rivers.

Similar Birds

Greater Scaup

Ring-necked Duck

Redhead

small, white wing patch and gray primaries

rear of crown forms a slight peak on head

tall, compressed head

white patch at base of bill

Nesting: does not nest in Kansas; nests in the northwestern U.S., Canada and Alaska; in tall, concealing vegetation, generally close to water, nest hollow is built of grass and lined with down; pale olive eggs are 2¼ x 1½ in; female incubates 8–10 eggs for about 25 days.

Did You Know?

The name "scaup" might be a phonetic imitation of one of its calls.

Look For

A member of the *Aythya* genus of diving ducks, the Lesser Scaup leaps up neatly before diving underwater, where it propels itself with powerful strokes of its feet.

Common Goldeneye
Bucephala clangula

The Common Goldeneye spends its entire life in North America, dividing its time between breeding grounds in the boreal forests of Canada and Alaska and wintering grounds in marine bays and estuaries along the Atlantic and Pacific coasts. Many also overwinter on large inland rivers, lakes and reservoirs, but numbers depend on food availability and open water. • Fish, crustaceans and mollusks make up a major portion of the Common Goldeneye's winter diet, but in summer, this diving duck eats aquatic invertebrates and tubers.

Other ID: golden eyes. *Male:* dark, iridescent green head; dark back; white sides and belly. *Female:* lighter breast and belly; gray-brown body plumage; dark bill is tipped with yellow in spring and summer.
Size: *L* 16–20 in; *W* 26 in.
Voice: generally silent in migration and winter. *Male:* courtship calls are a nasal *peent* and a hoarse *kraaagh. Female:* a harsh croak.
Status: common migrant and winter resident.
Habitat: open water of lakes, large ponds and rivers.

Similar Birds

Barrow's Goldeneye

Bufflehead

Hooded Merganser

black wings with large, white wing patches

♂

♀

chocolate brown head

steep forehead with peaked crown

dark bill

♀

white, oval cheek patch

♂

Nesting: does not nest in Kansas; nests in Canada and Alaska; in a tree cavity or occasionally a nest box lined with wood chips and down; often close to water; blue-green eggs are 2⅜ x 1⅝ in; female incubates 6–10 eggs for 28–32 days

Did You Know?

In winter, female Common Goldeneyes fly farther south than males, and juvenile birds continue even farther south.

Look For

When courting a female, a male will arch his head backward until his crown seems to touch his back and then catapult his head forward like a coiled spring.

Common Merganser
Mergus merganser

Lumbering like a jumbo jet, the Common Merganser must run along the surface of the water, beating its heavy wings to gain sufficient lift to take off. Once up and away, this large duck flies arrow-straight and low over the water, making broad, sweeping turns to follow the meandering shorelines of rivers and lakes.
• Common Mergansers are highly social and often gather in large groups during migration. In winter, any source of open water with a fish-filled shoal will support good numbers of these skilled divers. • Two close relatives also visit Kansas, the Red-Breasted Merganser and the Hooded Merganser.

Other ID: large, elongated body. *Male:* white body plumage; black stripe on back; dark eyes; blood red feet. *Female:* gray body; orange eyes. *In flight:* shallow wingbeats; body is compressed and arrowlike.
Size: *L* 22–27 in; *W* 34 in.
Voice: *Male:* harsh *uig-a*, like a guitar twang. *Female:* harsh *karr karr*.
Status: abundant migrant and winter resident on lakes with open water.
Habitat: large rivers and deep lakes.

Similar Birds

Red-breasted Merganser

Hooded Merganser

Common Goldeneye (p. 34)

glossy, green head without crest

blood red bill

♂

rusty neck and crested head

orange bill

♀

clean white "chin" and breast

Nesting: does not nest in Kansas; nests in Canada and the western U.S.; in a tree cavity; occasionally on the ground, on a cliff ledge or in a large nest box; usually close to water; pale buff eggs are 2½ x 1¾ in; female incubates 8–11 eggs for 30–35 days.

Did You Know?

The Common Merganser is the most widespread and abundant merganser in North America. It also occurs in Europe and Asia.

Look For

In flight, the Common Merganser has shallow wing beats and an arrowlike, compressed body.

Ring-necked Pheasant

Phasianus colchicus

The Ring-necked Pheasant was brought to North America from China in the late 1800s and was introduced to Kansas early in the 20th century. It soon became quite abundant, especially in the arid west, and is now considered to be our most desirable gamebird. • Unlike native grouse, the Ring-necked Pheasant does not have feathered legs and feet for insulation. It cannot live on native plants alone and depends on grain and corn crops for survival during severe winters.

Other ID: *Male:* bronze underparts. *Female:* mottled brown overall; light underparts.
Size: *Male:* L 30–36 in; W 31 in. *Female:* L 20–26 in; W 28 in.
Voice: *Male:* loud, raspy, rooster-like crowing: *ka-squawk;* whirring of the wings mostly just before sunrise.
Status: abundant year-round resident in western Kansas; common in central Kansas; rare in the southeastern part of the state.
Habitat: shrubby grasslands, hay fields, grassy ditches and fencelines, woodlots and occasionally croplands.

Similar Birds

Greater Prairie-Chicken (p.40)

Lesser Prairie-Chicken

Greater Roadrunner

naked, red face patch

green head

white collar

large, long, barred tail

♂

Nesting: on the ground, among vegetation or next to a log or other natural debris; in a slight depression lined with grass and leaves; olive buff eggs are 1¾ x 1⅜ in; female incubates 10–12 eggs for 23–28 days.

Did You Know?

Heard more often than seen, this bird's loud *ka-squawk* call resonates through farms, woodlots and brushy suburban parks.

Look For

The Ring-necked Pheasant does not fly long distances; it exhibits bursts of labored flight and then long glides, which allows it to escape most predators.

Greater Prairie-Chicken

Tympanuchus cupido

The mating display of the male Greater Prairie-Chicken, as it dances and "booms" and engages in mock combat, is an unforgettable and timeless sight on the Kansas prairie. Though prairie-chickens have declined and are now absent from much of their historical range, healthy populations of both Greater and Lesser prairie-chickens can still be found in southwestern Kansas.

♀

Other ID: fairly robust, open-country gamebird; pale forehead; pale throat.
Size: *L* 17 in; *W* 27–29 in. Males are larger than females.
Voice: male's low-frequency booming *whhooo-doo-dooohh* on lek is accompanied by foot-stamping, wing-shaking and tail-clicking; female utters low *kuk, kwerr* and *brirrb* calls.
Status: uncommon year-round resident.
Habitat: tall-grass prairies, taller grassy areas in prairies, farmlands and grain fields; prairie openings in oak woodlands, oak savannahs and riparian oak thickets.

Similar Birds

Lesser Prairie-Chicken

Ring-necked Pheasant,
female (p. 38)

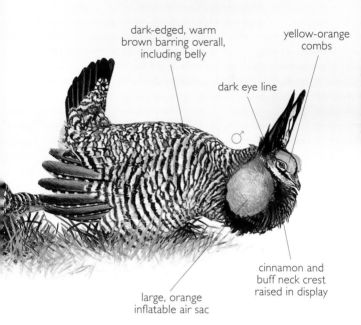

dark-edged, warm brown barring overall, including belly

yellow-orange combs

dark eye line

♂

cinnamon and buff neck crest raised in display

large, orange inflatable air sac

Nesting: female forms bowl-shaped depression and lines it with feathers, dried grass, leaves or small twigs; speckled, tawny olive eggs are 1¾ x 1⅜ in; female incubates 8–13 eggs for 23–25 days.

Did You Know?

Nearly 96 percent of native tall-grass prairie habitat has disappeared in North America, contributing to the decline of many birds that nest there.

Look For

The long, raised head feathers on the displaying male, which are said to resemble the wings of Cupid, inspired the species name *cupido*.

Wild Turkey
Meleagris gallopavo

The Wild Turkey was once common throughout most of eastern North America, but in the early 20th century, habitat loss and overhunting totally eliminated this bird from Kansas. Today, restoration efforts have reestablished the Wild Turkey throughout Kansas wherever there are small wooded tracts of land. • This charismatic bird is the only native North American animal that has been widely domesticated. The wild ancestors of most domestic animals came from Europe. • Early in life both male and female turkeys gobble. The females eventually outgrow this practice, leaving the males to gobble competitively for the honor of mating.

Other ID: largely unfeathered legs. *Male:* black-tipped breast feathers. *Female:* smaller; blue-gray head; less iridescent body; brown-tipped breast feathers.
Size: *Male: L* 3–3½ ft; W 5½ ft. *Female: L* 3 ft; W 4 ft.
Voice: courting male gobbles loudly; alarm call is a loud *pert;* gathering call is a cluck; contact call is a loud *keouk-keouk-keouk.*
Status: common year-round resident.
Habitat: deciduous, mixed and riparian woodlands; occasionally in farm fields in late fall and winter.

Look For

Eastern Wild Turkeys were reintroduced in eastern Kansas, but the smaller Rio Grande race was stocked in western Kansas; hybrids now thrive in central Kansas.

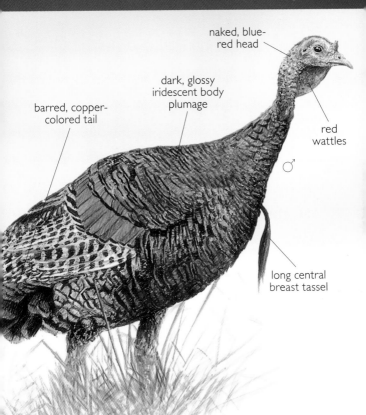

naked, blue-red head

dark, glossy iridescent body plumage

barred, copper-colored tail

red wattles

♂

long central breast tassel

Nesting: under thick cover in a woodland or at a field edge; in a depression on the ground, lined with vegetation; brown-speckled, pale buff eggs are 2½ x 1¾ in; female incubates 10–12 eggs for up to 28 days.

Did You Know?

If Congress had taken Benjamin Franklin's advice in 1782, our national emblem would be the Wild Turkey instead of the majestic Bald Eagle.

Northern Bobwhite
Colinus virginianus

The characteristic whistled *bob-white* call is heard throughout Kansas in spring. The male's well-known call is often the only evidence of this bird's presence among the dense, tangled vegetation of its rural, woodland home. • Throughout fall and winter, Northern Bobwhites typically travel in large family groups called coveys. When a predator approaches, the covey bursts into flight, creating a confusing flurry of activity. With the arrival of summer, breeding pairs break away from their coveys to perform elaborate courtship rituals in preparation for another nesting season.

Other ID: mottled brown, buff and black upperparts; white crescents and spots edged in black on chestnut brown sides and upper breast; short tail.
Size: *L* 10 in; *W* 13 in.
Voice: whistled *hoy*, given year-round. *Male:* a whistled, rising *bob-white* in spring and summer.
Status: common year-round resident in the eastern half of the state, less common in the west.
Habitat: farmlands, open woodlands, woodland edges, grassy fencelines, roadside ditches and brushy, open country.

Similar Birds

Scaled Quail

Look For

Bobwhites benefit from habitat disturbance and are often found in early succession habitats created by fire, agriculture and forestry.

broad, white eyebrow

buff throat and eyebrow

white throat

♂

♀

Nesting: in a shallow depression on the ground, often concealed by vegetation or a woven, partial dome; nest is lined with grass and leaves; white to pale buff eggs are 1¼ x 1 in; pair incubates 12–16 eggs for 22–24 days.

Did You Know?

Northern Bobwhites huddle together on cold winter nights, with each bird facing outward, enabling the group to detect danger from any direction.

Pied-billed Grebe
Podilymbus podiceps

Relatively solid bones and the ability to partially deflate its air sac allow the Pied-billed Grebe to sink below the surface of the water like a tiny submarine. The inconspicuous grebe can float low in the water or submerge with only its nostrils and eyes showing above the surface. • These grebes build their floating nests among sparse vegetation. When frightened by an intruder, they cover their eggs and slide underwater, leaving a nest that looks like nothing more than a mat of debris.

nonbreeding

Other ID: *Breeding:* white undertail coverts; pale belly. *Nonbreeding:* bill lacks black ring; white chin and throat; brownish crown.
Size: L 12–15 in; W 16 in.
Voice: loud, whooping call begins quickly, then slows down: *kuk-kuk-kuk cow cow cow cowp cowp cowp.*
Status: common migrant; rare summer resident.
Habitat: ponds, marshes and backwaters with sparse emergent vegetation.

Similar Birds

Eared Grebe   Horned Grebe   Western Grebe

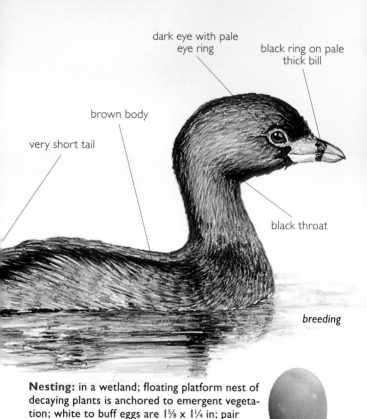

dark eye with pale eye ring

black ring on pale thick bill

brown body

very short tail

black throat

breeding

Nesting: in a wetland; floating platform nest of decaying plants is anchored to emergent vegetation; white to buff eggs are 1⅝ x 1¼ in; pair incubates 4–5 eggs for about 23 days and raises the striped young together.

Did You Know?

The scientific name *podiceps* means "rump foot," in reference to the way the bird's feet are located far back on its body.

Look For

Dark plumage, small size, individually webbed toes and a chicken-like bill distinguish the Pied-billed Grebe from other waterfowl.

American White Pelican
Pelecanus erythrorhynchos

This majestic wetland bird is one of only a few bird species that feeds cooperatively. A group of pelicans will herd fish into a school and then dip their bucket-like bills into the water to capture their prey. In a single scoop, a pelican can trap over 3 gallons of water and fish in its bill, which is about two to three times as much as its stomach can hold. This impressive feat inspired Dixon Lanier Merritt to write: "A wonderful bird is a pelican. His bill will hold more than his belican!" • Birds seen in winter are usually sick or injured.

Other ID: *Breeding:* small, keeled plate develops on upper mandible; pale yellow crest on back of head. *Nonbreeding* and *immature:* white plumage is tinged with brown.
Size: *L* 4½–6 ft; *W* 9 ft.
Voice: generally quiet; rarely issues piglike grunts.
Status: common migrant; rare summer resident.
Habitat: lakes; large rivers and marshes.

Similar Birds

Snow Goose
(p. 20)

Look For

The feathers on a pelican's wing tips are black and have a pigment called melanin that doesn't wear away in the wind.

short tail

nonbreeding

black primary and
secondary wing
feathers

naked orange skin
patch around eye

very large, stocky,
white bird

long, orange bill
and throat pouch

nonbreeding

Nesting: does not nest in Kansas; colonial; on
a bare, low-lying island; nest scrape is unlined or
lined with twigs; dull white eggs are 3⅜ x 2¼ in;
pair incubates 2 eggs for 29–36 days.

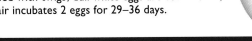

Did You Know?

American White Pelicans prefer to forage in shallow marshes,
rivers and lake edges. These birds eat about 4 pounds of fish
per day, but because they prefer nongame species, they do
not pose a threat to the potential catches of fishermen.

Double-crested Cormorant

Phalacrocorax auritus

The Double-crested Cormorant looks like a bird but smells and swims like a fish. With a long, rudderlike tail and excellent underwater vision, this slick-feathered bird has mastered the underwater world. Most water birds have waterproof feathers, but the structure of the Double-crested Cormorant's feathers allow water in. "Wettable" feathers make this bird less buoyant, which in turn makes it a better diver. The Double-crested Cormorant also has sealed nostrils for diving, and therefore must fly with its bill open.

Other ID: black body; blue eyes. *Nonbreeding:* no plumes trail from eyebrows. *Immature:* brown upperparts; buff throat and breast; yellowish throat patch. *In flight:* rapid wingbeats; kinked neck.
Size: *L* 26–32 in; *W* 4¼ ft.
Voice: generally quiet; may issue pig-like grunts or croaks, especially near nest colonies.
Status: common migrant; rare breeding species; rare in winter.
Habitat: large lakes and large, meandering rivers.

Similar Birds

Common Loon

Neotropic Cormorant

fine, black plumes trail from eyebrows

thin bill, hooked at tip

long, crooked neck

juvenile

orange-yellow throat pouch

breeding

Nesting: colonial; on an island or high in a tree; platform nest is made of sticks and guano; pale blue eggs are 2 x 1½ in; both sexes incubate 2–7 eggs for 25–30 days.

Did You Know?

Japanese fishermen sometimes use cormorants on leashes to catch fish. This traditional method of fishing is called *ukai*.

Look For

Double-crested Cormorants often perch on trees or piers with their wings partially spread. Lacking oil glands, they use the wind to dry their feathers.

Great Blue Heron
Ardea herodias

These herons are often mistakenly called cranes, but unlike cranes, which hold their necks outstretched in flight, herons fly with their long necks tucked toward their bodies. • Like most other wading birds, Great Blue Herons nest in colonies known as rookeries. These rookeries can contain dozens to thousands of pairs, usually among other species of water birds. They are usually located on isolated islands or in wooded swamps to avoid terrestrial predators such as raccoons. Nesting herons are sensitive to human disturbance, so observe these birds from a distance.

Other ID: large, blue-gray wading bird; long, dark legs; curved neck; plumes on throat. *In flight:* slow, steady wingbeats.
Size: L 4–4½ ft; W 6 ft.
Voice: deep *frahnk-frahnk-frahnk* when startled.
Status: common summer resident; uncommon in winter near open water.
Habitat: forages along the edges of various types of wetlands, from saline to freshwater; also stalks fields or yards.

Similar Birds

Tricolored Heron

Little Blue Heron

neck folds back over shoulders

black plumes above eye

large, straight, yellow bill

chestnut thighs

Nesting: colonial; stick platform up to 4 ft in diameter is built in a tree or shrub; pale blue-green eggs are 2½ x 1¾ in; pair incubates 3–7 eggs for 22–29 days.

Did You Know?

Although Great Blue Herons mostly feed on fish and other aquatic life, sometimes they can be seen feeding on rodents in fields and meadows.

Look For

The Great Blue Heron is the tallest of all herons and egrets in North America.

Great Egret
Ardea alba

The plumes of the Great Egret and Snowy Egret were widely used to decorate women's hats during the early 20th century. An ounce of egret feathers cost as much as $32—more than an ounce of gold at the time! As a result, egret populations rapidly plummeted toward extirpation. Some of the most successful conservation legislation in North America was enacted to outlaw the killing of the Great Egret and other birds for their plumes. Great Egret populations have recovered, and the birds now breed farther north than they did historically. • Egrets are named after their silky breeding plumes, called "aigrettes," which most species produce during courtship. The aigrettes of a Great Egret can grow up to 4½ feet long!

Other ID: large, all-white wading bird. *Nonbreeding:* yellow lores. *In flight:* slow wingbeats; neck folds back over shoulders; legs extend backward.
Size: *L* 3–3½ ft; *W* 4 ft.
Voice: generally silent away from colonies.
Status: common migrant; locally common summer resident.
Habitat: edges of marshes, lakes and ponds; flooded agricultural fields.

Similar Birds

Snowy Egret

Cattle Egret

Little Blue Heron, immature

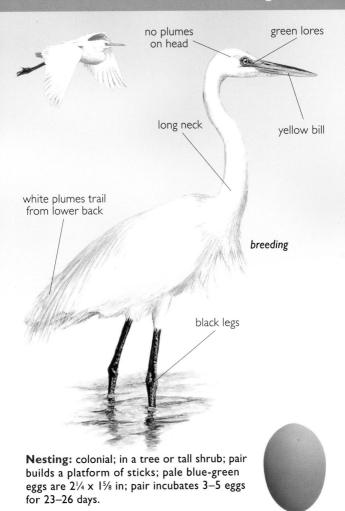

no plumes
on head

green lores

long neck

yellow bill

white plumes trail
from lower back

breeding

black legs

Nesting: colonial; in a tree or tall shrub; pair
builds a platform of sticks; pale blue-green
eggs are 2¼ x 1⅝ in; pair incubates 3–5 eggs
for 23–26 days.

Did You Know?

The Great Egret is the
symbol of the National
Audubon Society, one of
the nation's oldest conservation organizations.

Look For

Because of their long legs and
long neck, Great Egrets can
forage in deeper water than
other egrets.

Black-crowned Night-Heron

Nycticorax nycticorax

When dusk's long shadows shroud the marshes, the Black-crowned Night-Heron hunts in the marshy waters. This heron crouches motionless, using its large, light-sensitive eyes to spot prey lurking in the shallows.

• The Black-crowned Night-Heron breeds throughout much of the United States and is the most abundant heron in the world, occurring virtually worldwide.

• There is another night-heron in Kansas called the Yellow-crowned Night-Heron. It is gray overall and has a black head with a pale yellow crown and a white cheek patch.

Other ID: stocky body; black back; gray neck and wings; dull yellow legs; stout, black bill. *Nonbreeding:* no plumes.

Size: *L* 23–26 in; *W* 3½ ft.

Voice: deep, guttural *quark* or *wok,* often heard as the bird takes flight.

Status: common migrant; rare breeding species

Habitat: shallow cattail and bulrush marshes, lakeshores and along slow-flowing rivers.

Similar Birds

Yellow-crowned Night-Heron

Green Heron

American Bittern

feet protrude only slightly beyond tail in flight

juvenile

black cap with 2 white plumes

large, red eyes

white cheek

breeding

Nesting: colonial; in a tree or shrub; male gathers nest material; female builds a loose nest platform of twigs and sticks and lines it with finer materials; pale green eggs are 2¼ x 1 in; pair incubates 3–4 eggs for 21–26 days.

Did You Know?

Nycticorax, meaning "night raven," refers to this bird's distinctive nighttime calls.

Look For

This heron can sometimes be seen swimming, looking like a strange duck.

Turkey Vulture
Cathartes aura

Turkey Vultures are intelligent, playful and social birds. Groups live and sleep together in large trees, or "roosts." Some roost sites are over a century old and have been used by the same family of vultures for several generations. • The genus name *Cathartes* means "cleanser" and refers to this bird's affinity for carrion. Its red, featherless head may appear grotesque, but this adaptation allows the bird to stay relatively clean while feeding on messy carcasses. • The Black Vulture, found only in extreme southeastern Kansas, has a very short tail, a silvery patch on its wing tips and a black head.

Other ID: *Immature:* gray head. *In flight:* rocks from side to side when soaring.
Size: *L* 25–31 in; *W* 5½–6 ft.
Voice: generally silent; occasionally produces a hiss or grunt if threatened.
Status: common migrant and summer resident; rare in winter in southern Kansas.
Habitat: usually flies over open country, shorelines or roads, rarely over forests.

Similar Birds

Golden Eagle   Bald Eagle   Black Vulture
(p. 62)

wings are held in
a shallow "V"

silver gray flight
feathers

bare, red head

brownish overall

pale, hooked bill

Nesting: in a cave, crevice, log or among boulders; uses no nest material; darkly marked, dull white eggs are 2¾ x 2 in; pair incubates 2 eggs for up to 41 days.

Did You Know?

A threatened Turkey Vulture will play dead or throw up. The odor of its vomit repulses attackers, much like the odor of a skunk's spray does.

Look For

Vultures appear small headed compared to eagles, which have feathered heads.

Mississippi Kite
Ictinia mississippiensis

Most often seen in flight, the Mississippi Kite floats above the southern plains, flapping lazily but rarely gliding. This bird feeds on flying insects such as dragonflies, cicadas, beetles, and grasshoppers, which are plucked out of the air with the bird's feet and eaten while in flight. Occasionally it captures vertebrates, including bats, swallows and swifts. • Mississippi Kites were traditionally restricted to the southern states, but their breeding range is expanding northward, with spring or summer sightings now occurring to southern New England.

Other ID: chestnut at base of primaries often inconspicuous. *In flight:* gray overall; long wings and tail; short outermost primary feathers; male has white inner wing patches.
Size: *L* 14 in; *W* 3 ft.
Voice: generally silent; alarm call: *kee-kew, kew-kew*; call of fledgling an emphatic *three-beers*.
Status: common summer resident in south-central and southwest Kansas.
Habitat: wooded riparian areas, windbreaks, residential areas, golf courses and parks.

Similar Birds

Northern Harrier (p. 64)

Peregrine Falcon

Sharp-shinned Hawk

pale head

dark gray back
and wings

black tail

dark gray
underparts

♂

Nesting: in a tall tree; pair constructs a flimsy stick platform lined with leaves; bluish white eggs are 1⅝ x 2⅜ in; pair incubates 2 eggs for 30–32 days.

Did You Know?

In Kansas, kites disperse northward after the breeding season. Flocks can be seen returning south in early fall.

Look For

Kites feed buoyantly on the wing over Kansas towns, often eating cicadas. They may show aggressive behavior to humans and pets around nest sites in residential areas.

Bald Eagle
Haliaeetus leucocephalus

This majestic sea eagle hunts mostly fish and is often found near water. While soaring hundreds of feet high in the air, an eagle can spot fish swimming underwater and small rodents scurrying through the grass. Eagles also scavenge carrion and steal food from other birds. • Eagles are becoming more common as they recover from the pesticide poisoning of the mid-20th century. You can sometimes see scores of eagles around large Kansas reservoirs during winter. The first confirmed successful nesting of Bald Eagles in Kansas occurred in the 1990s, and more than 20 pairs of Bald Eagles currently nest in our state.

Other ID: *1st-year:* dark overall; dark bill; some white in underwings. *2nd-year:* dark "bib"; white in underwings. *3rd-year:* yellow at base of bill; yellow eyes. *4th-year:* light head with dark facial streak; variable pale and dark plumage; yellow eyes; paler eyes.
Size: L 30–43 in; W 5½–8 ft.
Voice: thin, weak squeal or gull-like cackle: *kleek-kik-kik-kik* or *kah-kah-kah*.
Status: common migrant and winter resident near open water; rare nesting species.
Habitat: near large lakes and rivers.

Similar Birds

Golden Eagle

Osprey

Turkey Vulture
(p. 58)

white head and tail

yellow bill

juvenile

yellow feet

Nesting: usually in a tree bordering a lake or large river; huge stick nest is often reused for many years; white eggs are 2¾ x 2⅛ in; pair incubates 1–3 eggs for 34–36 days.

Did You Know?

The Bald Eagle, a symbol of freedom, longevity and strength, became the national emblem of the United States in 1782.

Look For

Eagles and Turkey Vultures can be told apart at long distances. The wings of eagles are held flat as they soar, whereas Turkey Vultures hold their wings tilted up in a "V."

Northern Harrier

Circus cyaneus

With its prominent white rump and distinctive slightly upturned wings, the Northern Harrier may be the easiest raptor to identify in flight. Unlike other midsized birds, it often flies close to the ground, relying on sudden surprise attacks to capture prey. • The courtship flight of the Northern Harrier is a spectacle worth watching in spring. The male climbs almost vertically in the air, then stalls and plummets in a reckless dive toward the ground. At the last second, he saves himself with a hairpin turn that sends him skyward again.

Other ID: *Male:* bluish gray to silver gray upperparts; white underparts; indistinct tail bands, except for 1 dark subterminal band. *Female:* dark brown upperparts; streaky, brown and buff underparts. *In flight:* long wings and tail; black wing tips; white rump.
Size: *L* 16–24 in; *W* 3½–4 ft.
Voice: generally quiet; high-pitched *ke-ke-ke-ke-ke-ke* near the nest or during courtship.
Status: common migrant and winter resident; rare nesting species
Habitat: open country, including fields, wet meadows, cattail marshes, bogs and croplands.

Similar Birds

Rough-legged Hawk
(p. 72)

Red-tailed Hawk
(p. 70)

Ferruginous Hawk

facial disc

♀

♀

♂

yellow legs

long, dark-banded tail

Nesting: on the ground; usually in tall vegetation or on a raised mound; shallow depression is lined with grass, sticks and cattails; bluish white eggs are $1^{7}/_{8}$ x $1^{3}/_{8}$ in; female incubates 4–6 eggs for 30–32 days.

Did You Know?

Britain's Royal Air Force was so impressed by the Northern Harrier's maneuverability that it named the Harrier aircraft after this bird.

Look For

The Northern Harrier's owl-like, parabolic facial disc enhances its hearing, allowing this bird to hunt by sound as well as sight.

Cooper's Hawk
Accipiter cooperii

The Cooper's Hawk quickly changes the scene at a backyard bird feeder when it comes looking for a meal. European Starlings, American Robins and House Sparrows are among its favorite choices of prey.
• You might also spot this songbird scavenger hunting along forest edges. With the help of its long tail, short rounded wings and flap-and-glide flight, it is capable of maneuvering quickly at high speeds to snatch prey in mid-air. • There are two other accipiters in Kansas. The Sharp-shinned Hawk is smaller with a squared-off tail and a less distinct dark crown. The Northern Goshawk, a winter visitor, is larger with a prominent eye line.

Other ID: short, rounded wings; dark barring on pale undertail and underwings; blue-gray back; white terminal tail band.
Size: *Male: L 15–17 in; W 27–32 in.*
Female: L 17–19 in; W 32–37 in.
Voice: fast, woodpecker-like
cac-cac-cac-cac.
Status: common migrant and winter resident; uncommon nesting species.
Habitat: mixed woodlands, riparian woodlands, urban gardens with feeders.

Similar Birds

Sharp-shinned Hawk

Northern Goshawk

Merlin

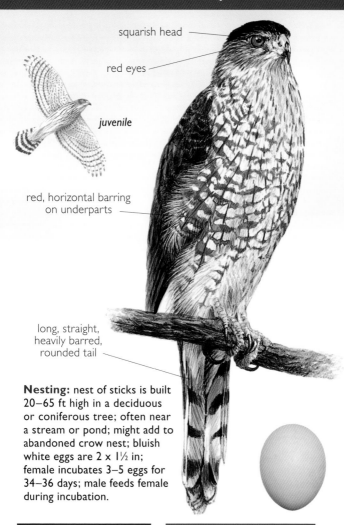

squarish head

red eyes

juvenile

red, horizontal barring
on underparts

long, straight,
heavily barred,
rounded tail

Nesting: nest of sticks is built
20–65 ft high in a deciduous
or coniferous tree; often near
a stream or pond; might add to
abandoned crow nest; bluish
white eggs are 2 x 1½ in;
female incubates 3–5 eggs for
34–36 days; male feeds female
during incubation.

Did You Know?

Female birds of prey are
always larger than the
males. The female
Cooper's Hawk hunts
birds as large as Rock
Pigeons.

Look For

Cooper's Hawks have been
known to run on the ground
for short distances when
chasing prey.

Swainson's Hawk
Buteo swainsoni

The Swainson's Hawk dominates the skies in the open, grassy expanses of Kansas where small rodents are abundant. It often follows tractors and is attracted to prairie fires. • Swainson's Hawks undertake long migratory journeys that may lead them from the southern tip of South America to as far north as Alaska. Traveling up to 12,500 miles in a single year, this hawk is second only to the arctic-breeding Peregrine Falcon for long-distance travel among birds of prey. • The massive "kettles" of Swainson's Hawks migrating through Central America have been likened to the legendary flocks of Passenger Pigeons that were said to blacken the sky.

Other ID: *Dark morph:* dark overall; brown wing linings blend with flight feathers. *Light morph:* white wing linings contrast with dark flight feathers.
Size: *L* 19–22 in; *W* 4½ ft.
Voice: typical hawk call, *keeeaar,* is higher pitched than a Red-tail's.
Status: common migrant and nesting species in western Kansas; uncommon migrant and rare nesting species in eastern Kansas; not present during winter.
Habitat: open fields, grasslands, sagebrush and agricultural areas.

Similar Birds

Red-tailed Hawk
(p. 70)

Red-shouldered Hawk

Broad-winged Hawk

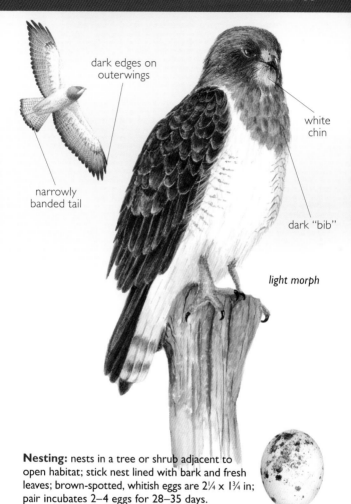

dark edges on outerwings

white chin

narrowly banded tail

dark "bib"

light morph

Nesting: nests in a tree or shrub adjacent to open habitat; stick nest lined with bark and fresh leaves; brown-spotted, whitish eggs are 2¼ x 1¾ in; pair incubates 2–4 eggs for 28–35 days.

Did You Know?

These hawks are occasionally seen in flocks of up to several hundred individuals in Kansas, especially in late September.

Look For

Pointed wing tips, slightly upturned wings and dark flight feathers differentiate the Swainson's Hawk from all other raptors in flight.

Red-tailed Hawk
Buteo jamaicensis

Take an afternoon drive through the country and look for Red-tailed Hawks soaring above the fields. Red-tails are the most common hawks in Kansas, especially in winter. • In warm weather, these hawks use thermals and updrafts to soar. The pockets of rising air provide substantial lift, which allows migrating hawks to fly for almost 2 miles without flapping their wings. On cooler days, resident Red-tails perch on exposed tree limbs, fence posts or utility poles to scan for prey.

Other ID: brown eyes; overall color varies geographically. *In flight:* light underwing flight feathers with faint barring; dark leading edge on underside of wings.
Size: *Male:* L 18–23 in; W 4–5 ft. *Female:* L 20–25 in; W 4–5 ft.
Voice: powerful, descending scream: *keeeearrrr.*
Status: common year-round resident, numbers increase during migration and in winter.
Habitat: open country with some trees; also roadsides or woodlots.

Similar Birds

Red-shouldered Hawk   Broad-winged Hawk   Swainson's Hawk
                                                          (p. 68)

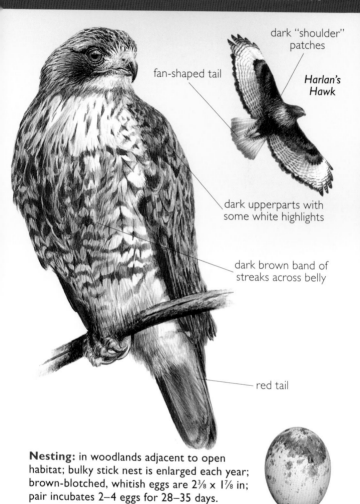

dark "shoulder" patches

Harlan's Hawk

fan-shaped tail

dark upperparts with some white highlights

dark brown band of streaks across belly

red tail

Nesting: in woodlands adjacent to open habitat; bulky stick nest is enlarged each year; brown-blotched, whitish eggs are 2⅜ x 1⅞ in; pair incubates 2–4 eggs for 28–35 days.

Did You Know?

The Red-tailed Hawk's piercing call is often paired with the image of an eagle in TV commercials and movies.

Look For

Courting pairs will dive at each other, lock talons and tumble toward the earth. They break away at the last second to avoid crashing into the ground.

Rough-legged Hawk
Buteo lagopus

Rough-legged Hawks appear on the central plains for a few short months each winter. When lemming and vole numbers are high on their Arctic breeding grounds, these hawks can produce up to seven young, resulting in many sightings in Kansas. Lean times in the Arctic often leads to fewer sightings here. • Rough-legged Hawks show great variety in coloration, ranging from a whitish light morph with dark patterning to dark-morph birds that are almost entirely dark with distinctive whitish areas. Both color morphs are found in Kansas.

Other ID: dark brown upperparts; dark streaks on head; light flight feathers. *Dark morph:* dark wing linings, head and underparts. *Immature:* lighter streaking on breast; bold belly band; buff leg feathers. *In flight:* most show dark "wrist" patches; frequently hovers.
Size: *L* 19–24 in; *W* 4–4½ ft.
Voice: alarm call is a catlike *kee-eer*, usually dropping at the end.
Status: uncommon migrant and winter resident
Habitat: fields, wet meadows, open bogs and agricultural croplands.

Similar Birds

Red-tailed Hawk
(p. 70)

Ferruginous Hawk

Northern Harrier
(p. 64)

dark streaks on breast

dark morph

white flight feathers with faint barring

wide, dark abdominal belt

legs are feathered to toes

light morph

Nesting: does not nest in Kansas; nests in the Arctic; large stick nest, possibly an abandoned raven nest; brownish blotched, bluish white eggs are 2¼ x 1¾ in; mostly female incubates 3–4 eggs for 28–31 days.

Did You Know?

The name *lagopus*, meaning "hare's foot," refers to this bird's distinctive feathered legs, which are an adaptation for survival in cold climates.

Look For

The Rough-legged Hawk often hovers in a stationary position, an adaptation that helps it hunt in open-country habitat, which often lacks high perches.

American Kestrel
Falco sparverius

The colorful American Kestrel, formerly known as the "Sparrow Hawk," is a common, widespread falcon, not shy of human activity and adaptable to habitat change. This small falcon has benefited from the grassy rights-of-way created by interstate highways, which provide habitat for grasshoppers and other small prey. Watch for this robin-sized bird along rural roadways, perched on poles and telephone wires, or hovering over agricultural fields, foraging for insects and small mammals. It is also found in cities, using industrial areas, vacant lots, landfills and highway interchanges for hunting rodents, large insects and even House Sparrows.

Other ID: lightly spotted underparts.
In flight: frequently hovers; buoyant, indirect flight style.
Size: L 7½–8 in; W 20–24 in.
Voice: usually silent; loud, often repeated, shrill *killy-killy-killy* when excited; female's voice is lower pitched.
Status: common year-round resident.
Habitat: open fields, woodlots, forest edges, roadside ditches, grassy highway medians, grasslands and croplands.

Similar Birds

Merlin

Peregrine Falcon

Prairie Falcon

2 distinctive facial stripes

long, rusty tail

rusty back and wings

blue-gray crown with rusty cap

♀

rusty breast streaking

blue-gray wings

♂

Nesting: in a tree cavity; may use a nest box; white to pale brown, speckled eggs are 1½ x 1⅛ in; mostly the female incubates 4–6 eggs for 29–30 days; both adults raise the young.

Did You Know?

The American Kestrel was the first falcon to reproduce by artificial insemination, and its observation has aided in studying the effects of pesticides on birds of prey.

Look For

The American Kestrel repeatedly lifts its tail while perched.

American Coot
Fulica americana

Though they resemble ducks, American Coots are actually more closely related to rails and galli-nules. Coots squabble constantly during the breeding season and can often be seen running along the surface of the water, splashing and charging at intruders. Outside of breeding season, coots gather in large amicable groups. During spring and fall, thousands congregate at a few staging areas in Kansas.
• With feet that have individually webbed toes, the coot can dive for underwater vegetation.

Other ID: red eyes; long, yellow-green legs; lobed toes; small, white marks on tail.
Size: L 13–16 in; W 24 in.
Voice: calls frequently in summer, day and night: *kuk-kuk-kuk-kuk-kuk*; also croaks and grunts.
Status: abundant migrant; rare summer and winter resident
Habitat: shallow marshes, ponds and wetlands with open water and emer-gent vegetation; also sewage lagoons.

Similar Birds

Pied-billed Grebe

Common Moorhen

Sora

reddish spot on white forehead shield

gray-black overall

white, chicken-like bill with dark ring around tip

Nesting: in emergent vegetation; pair builds floating nest of cattails and grass; buffy white, brown-spotted eggs are 2 x 1⅜"; pair incubates 8–12 eggs for 21–25 days; may raise 2 broods.

Did You Know?

American Coots, sometimes called "mudhens," are the most widespread and abundant rails in North America.

Look For

Many features distinguish a coot from a duck, including head-bobbing while swimming or walking, a narrower bill that extends up the forehead, and the lack of fully webbed feet.

Killdeer

Charadrius vociferus

The Killdeer is a gifted actor, well known for its "broken wing" distraction display. When an intruder wanders too close to its nest, the Killdeer greets the interloper with piteous cries while dragging a wing and stumbling about as if injured. Most predators take the bait and follow, and once the Killdeer has lured the predator far away from its nest, it miraculously recovers from its "injury" and flies off. • This shorebird is one of the first birds to return in spring, sometimes returning too soon and becoming a casualty of early spring snow and ice storms.

Other ID: brown head; white neck band; brown back and upperwings; white underparts; rufous rump. *Immature:* downy; only 1 breast band.
Size: L 9–11 in; W 24 in.
Voice: loud, distinctive *kill-dee kill-dee kill-deer;* variations include *deer-deer.*
Status: common summer resident; some linger into winter, particularly if the winter is mild.
Habitat: open areas, such as fields, lakeshores, sandy beaches, mudflats, gravel streambeds, wet meadows and grasslands.

Similar Birds

Semipalmated Plover

Piping Plover

Snowy Plover

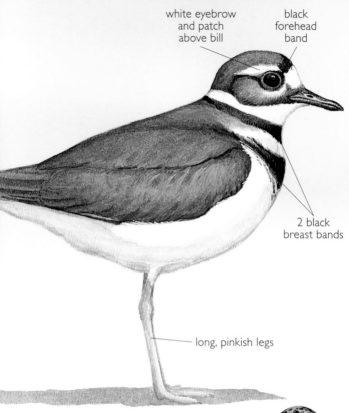

white eyebrow and patch above bill

black forehead band

2 black breast bands

long, pinkish legs

Nesting: on open ground, in a shallow, usually unlined depression; heavily marked, creamy buff eggs are 1⅜ x 1⅛ in; pair incubates 4 eggs for 24–28 days; may raise 2 broods.

Did You Know?

The European Starling can imitate the Killdeer's call.

Look For

The Killdeer has adapted well to urbanization, and it finds golf courses, farms, fields and abandoned industrial areas much to its liking.

Spotted Sandpiper
Actitis macularius

The female Spotted Sandpiper, unlike most other female birds, lays her eggs and leaves the male to tend to the clutch. She diligently defends her territory and may mate with several different males. Of the world's bird species, only about one percent display this unusual breeding strategy known as "polyandry." Each summer, the female may lay up to four clutches and is capable of producing 20 eggs. As the season progresses, however, available males become harder to find. Come August, there may be seven females for every available male.

Other ID: *Nonbreeding and immature:* pure white breast, foreneck and throat; brown bill; dull yellow legs. *In flight:* flies close to the water's surface with very rapid, shallow, stiff-winged strokes.
Size: *L* 7–8 in; *W* 15 in.
Voice: sharp, crisp *eat-wheat, eat-wheat, wheat-wheat-wheat-wheat.*
Status: common migrant; rare summer resident
Habitat: shorelines, gravel beaches, drainage ditches, swamps and sewage lagoons; occasionally seen in cultivated fields.

Similar Birds

Solitary Sandpiper

Dunlin

Sanderling

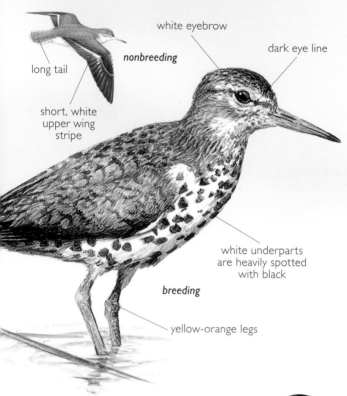

nonbreeding

long tail

short, white upper wing stripe

white eyebrow

dark eye line

white underparts are heavily spotted with black

breeding

yellow-orange legs

Nesting: usually near water; shallow scrape is lined with grass and sheltered by vegetation; darkly blotched, creamy buff eggs are 1¼ x 1 in; male incubates 4 eggs for 20–24 days.

Did You Know?

Sandpipers have four toes: three pointing forward and one pointing backward. Plovers, such as the Killdeer, have only three toes.

Look For

Spotted Sandpipers bob their tails constantly on shore and fly with rapid, shallow, stiff-winged strokes.

Lesser Yellowlegs
Tringa flavipes

The "tattletale" Lesser Yellowlegs is the self-appointed sentinel in a mixed flock of shorebirds, raising the alarm at the first sign of a threat.
• Differentiating Lesser Yellowlegs and Greater Yellowlegs in the field is challenging, but with practice you will notice that the Lesser's bill is finer, straighter and shorter, about as long as its head is wide. The Lesser is also more commonly seen in flocks. Finally, the Lesser Yellowlegs emits a pair of peeps, while the Greater Yellowlegs peeps three times. • In Kansas, fall migration for shorebirds begins in late July. Spring migration occurs mostly in April and May.

Other ID: subtle, dark eye line; pale lores.
Nonbreeding: grayer overall.
Size: L 10–11 in; W 24 in.
Voice: typically a high-pitched pair of *tew* notes; noisiest on breeding grounds.
Status: common migrant.
Habitat: shorelines of lakes, rivers, marshes and ponds.

Similar Birds

Willet

Greater Yellowlegs

Solitary Sandpiper

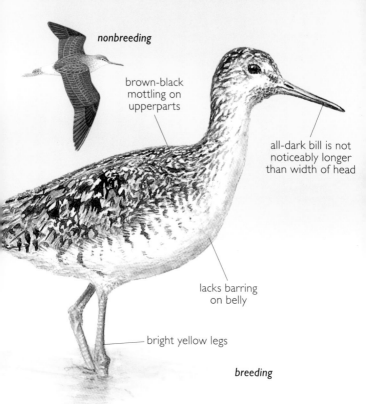

nonbreeding

brown-black mottling on upperparts

all-dark bill is not noticeably longer than width of head

lacks barring on belly

bright yellow legs

breeding

Nesting: does not nest in Kansas; nests in the Arctic; in a natural forest opening; in a depression on a dry mound lined with leaves and grass; darkly blotched, buff to olive eggs are 1⅝ x 1⅛ in; pair incubates 4 eggs for 22–23 days.

Did You Know?

Yellowlegs were popular game birds in the 1800s because they were plentiful and easy to shoot.

Look For

When feeding, the Lesser Yellowlegs wades into water almost to its belly, sweeping its bill back and forth just below the water's surface.

Baird's Sandpiper
Calidris bairdii

Migrating farther and faster than most birds, Baird's Sandpipers complete their 9300-mile journey from the High Arctic to the tip of South America in just 5 weeks. These modest-looking sandpipers remain on their northern breeding grounds for only a short time. As soon as the chicks hatch and are able to fend for themselves, the adults migrate to staging areas in the Canadian Prairies and northern Great Plains. There they refuel on insects for what is often a direct, nonstop journey to South America. Once the young accumulate fat reserves, they follow in a second wave of southbound migrants.

Other ID: *Breeding:* large, black, diamondlike patterns on back and wing coverts.
Size: L 7–7½ in; W 17 in.
Voice: soft, rolling *kriit kriit.*
Status: common migrant.
Habitat: sandy beaches, mudflats and wetland edges.

Similar Birds

Semipalmated
Sandpiper

Least Sandpiper

Pectoral Sandpiper

distinctive,
"scaly" back

black bill

folded wings
extend beyond tail

faint, buff brown
breast speckling

black legs

nonbreeding

Nesting: does not nest in Kansas; nests in the Arctic; on dry, sparsely vegetated tundra; in a shallow depression lined with grass; buff eggs, blotched with reddish brown are 1⅜ x 1 in; both adults incubate 4 eggs for 21 days.

Did You Know?

The Baird's Sandpiper invests more in egg production than most birds. The female lays four eggs that may total up to 120 percent of her body mass.

Look For

Baird's Sandpipers occasionally migrate with other sandpipers, but upon landing they will often leave the flock to feed alone.

Franklin's Gull

Larus pipixcan

The Franklin's Gull is not a typical "sea gull." This land-loving bird spends much of its life inland and nests on the prairies, where it is affectionately known as "Prairie Dove." It often follows tractors across agricultural fields, snatching up insects from the tractor's path in much the same way its cousins follow fishing boats. • Franklin's Gull is one of only a few gull species that migrate long distances between breeding and wintering grounds—the majority of Franklin's Gulls over-winter along the Pacific Coast of Peru and Chile.

Other ID: gray mantle; white underparts.
Nonbreeding: dark patch on back of whitish head; black legs.
Size: *L* 13–15 in; *W* 3 ft.
Voice: shrill, "mewing" *weeeh-ah weeeh-ah* while feeding and in migra-tion; also a shrill *kuk-kuk-kuk*.
Status: abundant migrant; very rare in summer and winter.
Habitat: agricultural fields, marshy lakes, landfills and large river and lakes.

Similar Birds

Bonaparte's Gull   Laughing Gull   Sabine's Gull

black crescent on
white wing tips

incomplete,
white eye ring

black head

nonbreeding

red-orange
bill

red-orange
legs

breeding

Nesting: does not nest in Kansas; nests in the
Canadian prairies and northern Great Plains; colonial; usually in dense emergent vegetation; floating
platform nest is built above water; variably
marked, pale greenish or buff eggs are 2 x 1⅜ in;
pair incubates 3 eggs for 25 days.

Did You Know?

This gull was named for Sir
John Franklin, the British
navigator and explorer
who led four expeditions
to the Canadian Arctic in
the 19th century.

Look For

Large flocks of Franklin's
Gulls numbering in the tens
of thousands linger on our
large reservoirs during fall
migration.

Ring-billed Gull

Larus delawarensis

Few people can claim that they have never seen this common, widespread gull. Highly tolerant of humans, Ring-billed Gulls are part of our everyday lives, scavenging our litter and frequenting our parks. These omnivorous gulls eat almost anything and swarm parks, beaches, golf courses and fast-food parking lots looking for food handouts, sometimes making pests of themselves. Few species have adjusted to human development as well as the Ring-billed Gull. • Seventeen different species of gulls have been found in Kansas. Most of these are rare fall or winter visitors to our large reservoirs.

Other ID: *Nonbreeding:* dark spotting on head.
In flight: pale gray mantle.
Size: L 18–20 in; W 4 ft.
Voice: high-pitched *kakakaka-akakaka;*
also a low, laughlike *yook-yook-yook.*
Status: common migrant; uncommon winter resident.
Habitat: lakes, rivers, landfills, golf courses, large parking lots, fields and parks.

Similar Birds

Herring Gull

Glaucous Gull

California Gull

white head

black ring around bill tip

yellow eyes

pale gray mantle

nonbreeding

white underparts

yellow legs

breeding

Nesting: does not nest in Kansas; nests in northern U.S. and Canada; colonial; in a shallow scrape on the ground, lined with grass, debris and small sticks; brown-blotched, gray to olive eggs are 2⅜ x 1⅝ in; pair incubates 2–4 eggs for 23–28 days.

Did You Know?

In chaotic nesting colonies, adult Ring-billed Gulls will call out and recognize the response of their chicks.

Look For

To differentiate between gulls, pay attention to the markings on their bills, the pattern of the wing tips and the color of their legs and eyes.

Forster's Tern
Sterna forsteri

In breeding plumage, the Forster's Tern so closely resembles the Common Tern that the two often seem indistinguishable. Look closely and you will notice that the Forster's bill is orange, whereas the Common's bill is darker red. In flight the Forester's wings have white trailing edges whereas the Common's are dark. • Forster's Tern has an exclusively North American breeding distribution, but it bears the name of a man who never visited this continent—German naturalist Johann Reinhold Forster (1729–98). Forster examined tern specimens sent to England from Hudson Bay, Canada, and was the first to recognize this bird as a distinct species.

Other ID: light gray mantle; white rump.
Nonbreeding: white head with black band through eyes; black bill. *In flight:* forked tail; long, pointed wings.
Size: L 14–16 in; W 31 in.
Voice: flight call is a nasal, short *keer keer;* also a grating *tzaap.*
Status: common migrant; rare summer resident.
Habitat: coastal areas; brackish wetlands; freshwater lakes, rivers and marshes.

Similar Birds

Caspian Tern   Black Tern   Least Tern

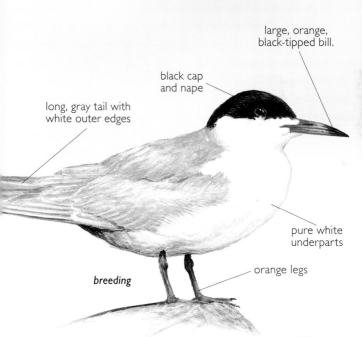

large, orange,
black-tipped bill.

black cap
and nape

long, gray tail with
white outer edges

pure white
underparts

orange legs

breeding

Nesting: has nested at Cheyenne Bottoms and Quivira NWR; builds a platform of floating vegetation in freshwater or saltwater marshes; olive to buff, blotched eggs are 1⅝ x 1¼ in; pair incubates 2–3 eggs for 24 days.

Did You Know?

The Forster's Tern's bill color changes from black in winter to orange with a black tip in summer.

Look For

Like most terns, the Forster's Tern catches fish in dramatic headfirst dives but also snatches flying insects in midair with graceful swoops, twists and turns.

Rock Pigeon
Columba livia

Rock Pigeons are familiar to anyone who has lived in the city. These colorful, acrobatic, seed-eating birds frequent parks, town squares, railroad yards and factory sites. Their tolerance of humans has made them a source of entertainment, as well as a pest. • This pigeon is likely a descendant of a Eurasian bird that was first domesticated about 4500 BC. Settlers introduced the Rock Pigeon to North America in the 17th century. • "Homing Pigeons" carried strategic messages during WWII, which saved hundreds of lives.

Other ID: usually has orange feet. *In flight:* holds wings in a deep "V" while gliding; white rump on most birds.
Size: *L* 12–13 in; *W* 28 in (male is usually larger).
Voice: soft, cooing *coorrr-coorrr-coorrr.*
Status: common year-round resident.
Habitat: urban areas, railroad yards and agricultural areas.

Similar Birds

Eurasian Collared-
Dove (p. 94)

Look For

No other "wild" bird varies as much in coloration, a result of semi-domestication and extensive inbreeding over time.

color is highly variable (iridescent blue-gray, red, white or tan)

white cere

Nesting: in a barn or on a cliff, bridge or tower; in a flimsy nest of sticks, grass and other vegetation; glossy white eggs are 1½ x 1⅛ in; pair incubates 2 eggs for 16–19 days; may raise broods year-round.

Did You Know?

These birds are some of the most well studied birds in the world. Much of our understanding of bird migration, endocrinology, color genetics and sensory perception comes from experiments involving Rock Pigeons.

Eurasian Collared-Dove

Streptopelia decaocto

The colonization of North America by Eurasian Collared-Doves is an astonishing story. Perhaps 50 of these doves were released in the Bahamas in 1974. They probably reached southeastern Florida that same decade, but because they so closely resemble the domestic Ringed Turtle-Dove, they were overlooked. They were finally "discovered" on the North American mainland in 1986. Eurasian Collared-Doves have now spread across much of the continent and are rapidly increasing. Colonization of Central and South America can be expected.
• *Streptopelia* is Greek for "twisted dove."

Other ID: large, chunky dove; square tail with white outer tail feathers.
Size: L 12–13 in; W 18–20 in.
Voice: a low *coo-Coo-coo*, repeated incessantly throughout the day.
Status: common year-round in Kansas towns; more common in western Kansas.
Habitat: primarily associated with humans; urban and suburban areas.

Similar Birds

Mourning Dove (p. 96)

Rock Pigeon (p. 92)

White-winged Dove

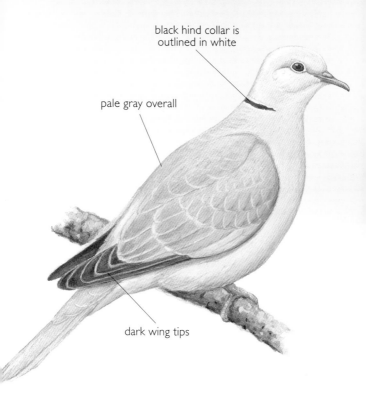

black hind collar is
outlined in white

pale gray overall

dark wing tips

Nesting: in a tree; female builds a platform of
twigs and sticks; white eggs are 1¼ x ⅞ in; pair
incubate 2 eggs for about 14 days; may raise
3 or more broods in a season.

Did You Know?

Native to India and southeast Asia, these doves dramatically expanded their
range during the 20th century to include other parts
of Asia, Europe and Africa.

Look For

These doves feed on grain
and are frequently seen near
grain elevators and at bird
feeders.

Mourning Dove
Zenaida macroura

The Mourning Dove's soft cooing, which filters through broken woodlands and suburban parks, is often confused with the sound of a hooting owl. Beginning birders who track down the source of the calls are often surprised to find the stream-lined silhouette of a perched dove. • This popular game bird is common throughout Kansas and is one of the most abundant native birds in North America. Human development has proven beneficial to this species by providing more open habitats and a variety of new food sources.

Other ID: buffy, gray-brown plumage; small head; dark bill; sleek body; dull red legs.
Size: *L* 11–13 in; *W* 18 in.
Voice: mournful, soft, slow *oh-woe-woe-woe.*
Status: common migrant and summer resident; less common in winter.
Habitat: open and riparian woodlands, forest edges, agricultural and suburban areas, open parks.

Similar Birds

White-winged Dove

Eurasian Collared-Dove (p. 94)

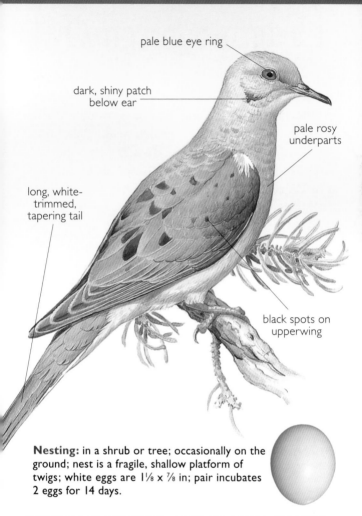

pale blue eye ring

dark, shiny patch below ear

pale rosy underparts

long, white-trimmed, tapering tail

black spots on upperwing

Nesting: in a shrub or tree; occasionally on the ground; nest is a fragile, shallow platform of twigs; white eggs are 1⅛ x ⅞ in; pair incubates 2 eggs for 14 days.

Did You Know?

The Mourning Dove raises up to six broods each year—more than any other native bird.

Look For

When the Mourning Dove bursts into flight, its wings clap above and below its body. It also often creates a whistling sound as it flies at high speed.

Eastern Screech-Owl
Megascops asio

The small Eastern Screech-Owl is a year-round resident of low-elevation, deciduous woodlands, though its presence is rarely detected. Screech-owls usually sleep away the daylight hours, but the excited calls from a mobbing horde of chickadees or a squawking gang of Blue Jays can alert you to an owl's presence. Small birds that mob a screech-owl often do so after losing a family member during the night. • Unique among Kansas owls, Eastern Screech-Owls show both red and gray color morphs. In Kansas, the gray morph is more common. • Western Screech Owls have recently been found along the Cimarron River near the border with Colorado. They are best identified by their different calls.

Other ID: reddish or grayish overall; yellow eyes.
Size: *L* 8–9 in; *W* 20–22 in.
Voice: horselike "whinny" that rises and falls plus a monotone trill.
Status: common year-round resident.
Habitat: mature deciduous forests, open deciduous and riparian woodlands, orchards and shade trees with natural cavities.

Similar Birds

Northern Saw-whet Owl

Long-eared Owl

Western Screech-Owl

short "ear" tufts

dark breast streaking

gray morph

Nesting: in a natural cavity or artificial nest box; no lining is added; white eggs are 1½ x 1⅜ in; female incubates 4–5 eggs for about 26 days; male brings food to the female during incubation.

Did You Know?

Screech-owls have one of the most varied diets of any owl and capture small animals, earthworms, insects and even fish.

Look For

Eastern Screech-Owls respond readily to whistled imitations of their calls, and sometimes several owls will appear to investigate the fraudulent perpetrator.

Great Horned Owl
Bubo virginianus

This highly adaptable and superbly camouflaged hunter has sharp hearing and powerful vision that allow it to hunt at night as well as by day. It will swoop down from a perch onto almost any small creature that moves. • An owl has specially designed feathers on its wings to reduce noise. The leading edge of the flight feathers is fringed rather than smooth, which interrupts airflow over the wing and allows the owl to fly silently. • Great Horned Owls begin their courtship as early as January, and by February and March the females are already incubating their eggs.

Other ID: overall plumage varies from light gray to dark brown; heavily mottled, gray, brown and black upperparts; yellow eyes; white chin.
Size: L 18–25 in; W 3–5 ft.
Voice: breeding call is 4–6 deep hoots: *hoo-hoo-hoooo hoo-hoo* or *Who's awake? Me too;* female gives higher-pitched hoots.
Status: common year-round resident.
Habitat: fragmented forests, fields, riparian woodlands, suburban parks and wooded edges of clearings.

Similar Birds

Long-eared Owl

Short-eared Owl

tall, widely spaced "ear" tufts form a triangle with bill

rusty orange facial disc is outlined in black

fine, horizontal barring on breast

Nesting: in another bird's abandoned stick nest or in a tree cavity; adds little or no nest material; dull whitish eggs are 2¼ x 1⅞ in; mostly the female incubates 2–3 eggs for 28–35 days.

Did You Know?

The Great Horned Owl has a poor sense of smell, which might explain why it is the only consistent predator of skunks.

Look For

Owls regurgitate pellets that contain the indigestible parts of their prey. You can find these pellets, which are generally clean and dry, under frequently used perches.

Barred Owl
Strix varia

The adaptable Barred Owl is found in large tracts of mature forest, ranging from swampy bottomlands to higher, mixed forests. • Each spring, the escalating laughs, hoots and gargling howls of Barred Owls reinforce pair bonds. They tend to be most vocal during late evening and early morning when the moon is full, the air is calm and the sky is clear. • Other owls lacking ear tufts can be found in Kansas, but they can easily be distinguished from the Barred Owl by differences in appearance and habitat.

Other ID: mottled, dark gray-brown plumage.
Size: *L* 17–24 in; *W* 3½–4 ft.
Voice: loud, hooting, rhythmic, laughing call is heard mostly in spring: *Who cooks for you? Who cooks for you all?*
Status: common year-round resident in eastern half of Kansas; very rare in western Kansas.
Habitat: mature forests, especially in dense stands near streams, rivers and lakes.

Similar Birds

Burrowing Owl　　　　Barn Owl　　　　Snowy Owl

no "ear" tufts

dark eyes

horizontal barring around neck and upper breast

pale bill

vertical streaking on belly

Nesting: in a natural tree cavity, broken tree-top or abandoned stick nest; adds very little material to the nest; white eggs are 2 x 1⅝ in; female incubates 2–3 eggs for 28–33 days.

Did You Know?

In darkness, the Barred Owl's eyesight may be 100 times keener than that of humans, and it is able to locate and follow prey using sound alone.

Look For

Dark eyes make the Barred Owl unique—most familiar large owls in North America have yellow eyes.

Common Nighthawk
Chordeiles minor

The Common Nighthawk makes an unforgettable booming sound as it flies high overhead. In an energetic courting display, the male dives, then swerves skyward, making a hollow *vroom* sound with his wings. • Like other members of the nightjar family, the Common Nighthawk has adapted to catch insects in midair: its large, gaping mouth is surrounded by feather shafts that funnel insects into its bill. A nighthawk can eat over 2600 insects in one day, including mosquitoes, blackflies and flying ants. • Look for nighthawks foraging for insects at nighttime baseball games.

Other ID: *Male:* white throat. *Female:* buffy throat.
In flight: shallowly forked, barred tail; erratic flight.
Size: L 8–10 in; W 23–26 in.
Voice: frequently repeated, nasal
peent peent.
Status: common summer resident.
Habitat: *Breeding:* forest openings, bogs, rocky outcroppings and gravel rooftops. *In migration:* over any area with large numbers of flying insects.

Similar Birds

Chuck-will's-widow

Whip-poor-will

Common Poorwill

bold, white "wrist" patches on long, pointed wings

very small bill

cryptic, mottled plumage

barred underparts

Nesting: on bare ground; no nest is built; heavily marked, creamy white to buff eggs are 1⅛ x ⅞ in; female incubates 2 eggs for about 19 days; both adults feed the young.

Did You Know?

It was once believed that members of the nightjar, or "goatsucker," family could suck milk from the udders of goats, causing the goats to go blind!

Look For

With their short legs and tiny feet, Nighthawks sit lengthwise on tree branches and blend in perfectly with the bark.

Chimney Swift

Chaetura pelagica

Chimney Swifts are the "frequent fliers" of the bird world—they feed, drink, bathe, collect nest material and even mate while they fly! They spend much of their time catching insects in the skies, high above the treetops. During night migrations, swifts sleep as they fly, relying on changing wind conditions to steer them. • Chimney Swifts have small, weak legs and cannot take flight again if they land on the ground. For this reason, swifts usually cling to vertical surfaces with their strong claws.

Other ID: brown overall; slim body.
In flight: rapid wingbeats; boomerang-shaped profile; erratic flight pattern.
Size: L 5–5½ in; W 12–13 in.
Voice: call is a rapid *chitter-chitter-chitter*, given in flight; also gives a rapid series of staccato *chip* notes.
Status: common summer resident.
Habitat: forages above cities and towns; roosts and nests in chimneys; may nest in tree cavities in more remote areas.

Similar Birds

Northern Rough-winged Swallow

Bank Swallow

Cliff Swallow
(p. 146)

long, thin, pointed, crescent-shaped wings

square tail

Nesting: often colonial; half-saucer nest of short twigs is attached to a vertical wall using saliva; white eggs are ¾ x ½ in; pair incubates 4–5 eggs for 19–21 days.

Did You Know?

Migrating Chimney Swifts may fly as high as 10,000 feet; above this altitude aircraft are required to carry oxygen.

Look For

In early evenings during migration, Chimney Swifts are often seen in high numbers, swirling above large, old chimneys before they enter to roost for the night.

Ruby-throated Hummingbird

Archilochus colubris

Ruby-throated Hummingbirds feed on sweet, energy-rich flower nectar, and they pollinate flowers in the process. You can attract humming-birds to your backyard with a red nectar feeder filled with a sugarwater solution (red food coloring is both unnecessary and harmful to the birds) or with tubular, nectar-producing flowers such as honeysuckle or bee balm. • Ruby-throated Hummingbirds migrate across the Gulf of Mexico—a nonstop, 500-mile journey.

Other ID: thin, needlelike bill; pale underparts.
Size: L 3½–4 in; W 4–4½ in.
Voice: a loud chick and other high squeaks; soft buzzing of the wings while in flight.
Status: common migrant and summer resident.
Habitat: open, mixed woodlands, wetlands, orchards, tree-lined mead-ows, flower gardens and backyards with trees and feeders.

Similar Birds

Black-chinned
Hummingbird

Broad-tailed
Hummingbird

Rufous Hummingbird

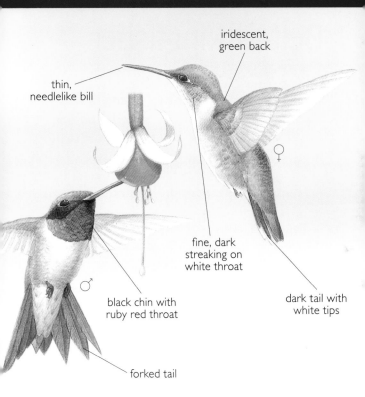

thin,
needlelike bill

iridescent,
green back

♀

fine, dark
streaking on
white throat

black chin with
ruby red throat

♂

dark tail with
white tips

forked tail

Nesting: on a horizontal tree limb; tiny, deep cup nest of plant down and fibers is held together with spider silk; lichens and leaves are pasted on the exterior walls; white eggs are ½ x ⅜ in; female incubates 2 eggs for 13–16 days.

Did You Know?

In straight-ahead flight, hummingbirds beat their wings up to 80 times per second, and their hearts can beat up to 1200 times per minute!

Look For

Weighing about as much as a nickel, hummingbirds can briefly reach speeds of up to 60 miles per hour and are the only birds that can fly backwards.

Belted Kingfisher
Ceryle alcyon

Perched on a bare branch over a productive pool, the Belted Kingfisher utters a scratchy, rattling call. Then, with little regard for its scruffy hairdo, it plunges headfirst into the water, snatching a fish or a frog. Back at its perch, the kingfisher flips its prey into the air and swallows it headfirst. Similar to owls, kingfishers regurgitate the indigestible portion of their food as pellets, which can be found beneath favorite perches. • Nestlings have closed eyes and are featherless for the first week, but after five days they are able to swallow small fish whole.

Other ID: bluish upperparts; small, white patch near eye; straight bill; short legs; white underwings.
Size: *L* 11–14 in; *W* 20–21 in.
Voice: fast, repetitive, cackling rattle, like a teacup shaking on a saucer.
Status: common summer resident and migrant; rare in winter near open water.
Habitat: rivers, large streams, lakes, marshes and ponds, especially near exposed soil banks, gravel pits or bluffs.

Similar Birds

Blue Jay
(p. 134)

Look For

With an extra reddish brown band across her belly, the female kingfisher is more colorful than her mate is.

shaggy crest

white collar

♀

blue-gray
breast band

♂

rust-colored belt
on female may be
incomplete

Nesting: in a cavity at the end of an earth
burrow; glossy white eggs are 1⅜ x 1 in; pair
incubates 6–7 eggs for 22–24 days.

Did You Know?

In Greek mythology, Alcyon, the daughter of the wind
god, grieved so deeply for her drowned husband that the gods
transformed them both into kingfishers.

Red-headed Woodpecker

Melanerpes erythrocephalus

This bird of the East lives mostly in open deciduous woodlands, urban parks and oak savannahs. Red-heads were once common throughout their range, but their numbers have declined dramatically over the past century. Since the introduction of the European Starling, Red-headed Woodpeckers have been largely outcompeted for nesting cavities. Also, these birds are frequent traffic fatalities, often struck by vehicles when they dart from their perches and over roadways to catch flying insects.

Other ID: black tail; white underparts.
Juvenile: brown head, back, wings and tail; slight brown streaking on white underparts.
Size: L 9–9½ in; W 17 in.
Voice: loud series of *kweer* or *kwrring* notes; occasionally a chattering *kerr-r-ruck;* also drums softly in short bursts.
Status: common summer resident and migrant; uncommon in winter.
Habitat: open deciduous woodlands (especially those with oak trees), urban parks, river edges and roadsides with groves of scattered trees.

Similar Birds

Pileated Woodpecker

Look For

Many woodpeckers have zygodactyl feet—two toes point forward and two point back—which allows them to move vertically up and down tree trunks.

bright red head

black back and wings

white rump and inner wing patches

juvenile

Nesting: male excavates a nest cavity in a dead tree or limb; white eggs are 1 x ¾ in; pair incubates 4–5 eggs for 12–13 days; both adults feed the young.

Did You Know?

Unlike other bird species, most male woodpeckers, including the Red-headed, incubate their eggs at night. Both parents may take turns incubating during the day.

Red-bellied Woodpecker
Melanerpes carolinus

The Red-bellied Woodpecker is no stranger to suburban backyards and will sometimes nest in birdhouses. This widespread bird is found year-round in woodlands throughout the eastern states, but numbers fluctuate depending on habitat availability and weather conditions. • Unlike most woodpeckers, Red-bellies consume large amounts of plant material such as berries and seeds, seldom excavating wood for insects. • When occupying an area together with Red-headed Woodpeckers, Red-bellies will nest in the trunk, below the foliage, and the Red-heads will nest in dead branches among the foliage.

Other ID: reddish tinge on belly. *Juvenile:* dark gray crown; streaked breast.
Size: L 9–10½ in; W 16 in.
Voice: call is a soft, rolling *churr;* drums in second-long bursts.
Status: common year-round resident.
Habitat: mature deciduous woodlands; occasionally in wooded residential areas.

Similar Birds

Northern Flicker
(p. 118)

Yellow-bellied
Sapsucker

black and white barring on back

red nape extends to forehead

♂

red nape

♀

white patch on rump is speckled with black

Nesting: in a cavity excavated mainly by the male; in woodlands or residential areas; white eggs are 1 x ¾ in; pair incubates 4–5 eggs for 12–14 days.

Did You Know?

Studies of banded Red-bellied Woodpeckers have shown that these birds have a life span in the wild of more than 20 years.

Look For

This woodpecker's namesake, its red belly, is only a small reddish area that is difficult to see in the field.

Downy Woodpecker

Picoides pubescens

A bird feeder well stocked with peanut butter and black-oil sunflower seeds may attract a pair of Downy Woodpeckers to your backyard. These approachable little birds are more tolerant of human activity than most other species, and they visit feeders more often than the larger, more aggressive Hairy Woodpeckers. • Like other woodpeckers, the Downy has evolved special features to help cushion the shock of repeated hammering, including a strong bill and neck muscles, a flexible, reinforced skull and a brain that is tightly packed in its protective cranium.

Other ID: black eye line and crown; white belly. *Male:* small, red patch on back of head. *Female:* no red patch.
Size: *L* 6–7 in; *W* 12 in.
Voice: long, unbroken trill; calls are a sharp *pik* or *ki-ki-ki* or whiny *queek queek*.
Status: common year-round resident.
Habitat: any wooded environment, especially deciduous and mixed forests and areas with tall, deciduous shrubs.

Similar Birds

Hairy Woodpecker

Ladder-backed Woodpecker

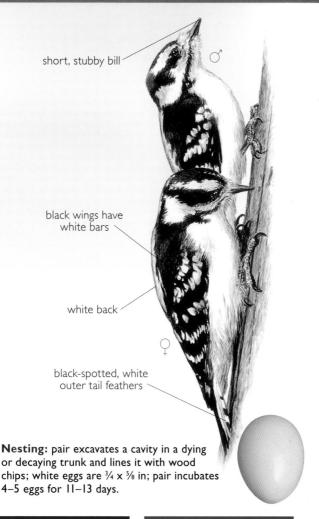

short, stubby bill

♂

black wings have
white bars

white back

♀

black-spotted, white
outer tail feathers

Nesting: pair excavates a cavity in a dying
or decaying trunk and lines it with wood
chips; white eggs are ¾ x ⅝ in; pair incubates
4–5 eggs for 11–13 days.

Did You Know?

Woodpeckers have feath-
ered nostrils, which filter
out the sawdust produced
by hammering.

Look For

The Downy Woodpecker has
several dark spots on its
white outer tail feathers,
whereas the larger Hairy
Woodpecker has outer tail
feathers that are pure white.

Northern Flicker
Colaptes auratus

Instead of boring holes in trees, the Northern Flicker scours the ground in search of invertebrates, particularly ants. With robinlike hops, it investigates anthills, grassy meadows and forest clearings. • Flickers often bathe in dusty depressions. The dust particles absorb oils and bacteria that can harm the birds' feathers. To clean themselves even more thoroughly, flickers squash ants and preen themselves with the remains. Ants contain formic acid, which kills small parasites on the birds' skin and feathers. • Red-shafted flickers can be found in the late fall and winter, particularly in western Kansas.

Other ID: long bill; gray crown; black-spotted, buff to whitish underparts; white rump. *Male:* black "mustache" stripe. *Female:* no "mustache."
Size: *L* 12–13 in; *W* 20 in.
Voice: loud, rapid, laughlike *kick-kick-kick-kick-kick-kick; woika-woika-woika* issued during courtship.
Status: common migrant and summer resident; uncommon in winter
Habitat: *Breeding:* open woodlands and forest edges, fields, meadows, golf courses, parks and gardens.

Similar Birds

Red-bellied
Woodpecker

Yellow-bellied
Sapsucker

brown, black-barred back and wings

♂ brownish to buff face

red nape crescent

black "bib" ♀

yellow underwings and undertail

Yellow-shafted

Nesting: pair excavates a cavity in a dying or decaying trunk and lines it with wood chips; may also use a nest box; white eggs are 1⅛ x ⅞ in; pair incubates 5–8 eggs for 11–16 days.

Did You Know?

The long tongue of a woodpecker wraps around twin structures in the skull and is stored like a measuring tape in its case.

Look For

Flickers in eastern North America have yellow under-wings and undertail coverts, whereas these are reddish in the red-shafted form found in the West.

Least Flycatcher
Empidonax minimus

The Least Flycatcher is the most common migrant *Empidonax* in Kansas and the only one that most birders confidently identify based on plumage alone. Its bold, white eye ring and white wing bars stand out at close view. Like many other flycatchers, these little birds are olive brown above and pale below, but they lack the obvious yellow tones of other flycatchers. Their call is a clear, sharp *whit*. • Though these flycatchers do not nest in Kansas, their conspicuous, two-part *che-bek* call can be heard in spring as they migrate northward. • Nine species of *Empidonax* flycatchers have been found in Kansas. The best way to identify them is by their vocalizations.

Other ID: white throat; olive brown upperparts; gray breast; gray white to yellowish belly and undertail coverts.
Size: L 4½–5½ in; W 7½–8 in.
Voice: *Male:* song is a constantly repeated, dry *che-bek che-bek*.
Status: common migrant.
Habitat: open deciduous or mixed woodlands; forest openings and edges; often in second-growth woodlands and occasionally near human habitation.

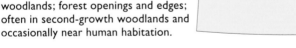

Similar Birds

Eastern Wood-Pewee

Acadian Flycatcher

Willow Flycatcher

bold, white
eye ring

2 white wing
bars

mostly dark bill
has yellow-orange
lower base

fairly long,
narrow tail

Nesting: does not nest in Kansas; nests in
northern U.S. and Canada; in the crotch or fork
of a small tree or shrub, often against the trunk;
female builds a small cup nest of plant fibers and
bark; creamy white eggs are ⅝ x ½ in; female
incubates 4 creamy white eggs for 13–15 days.

Did You Know?

Empidonax flycatchers are
aptly named: the literal
translation is "mosquito
king" and refers to their
insect-hunting prowess.

Look For

A feeding flycatcher will sit
on a branch, dart out suddenly to snap up an insect,
and then circle back to land
on the same perch.

Eastern Phoebe
Sayornis phoebe

Whether you are poking around a barnyard,
a campground picnic shelter or your backyard shed,
there is a very good chance you will happen upon
an Eastern Phoebe family and their marvelous
mud nest. The Eastern Phoebe's nest building and
territorial defense is normally well underway by
the time most other nesting songbirds arrive in
Kansas in late April and May. Once limited to
nesting on natural cliffs and fallen riparian trees,
this adaptive flycatcher has found success nesting
in culverts and under bridges and eaves, especially
when water is near. Look for them around such
structures.

Other ID: gray-brown upperparts; belly may
be washed with yellow in fall; no eye ring; weak
wing bars; dark legs.
Size: L 6½–7 in; W 10½ in.
Voice: *Male:* song is a hearty, snappy *fee-bee*,
delivered frequently; call is a sharp *chip*.
Status: common breeding species and
migrant; less common in western Kansas.
Habitat: open deciduous woodlands,
forest edges and clearings; usually near
water.

Similar Birds

Eastern Wood-Pewee

Yellow-bellied
Flycatcher

Say's Phoebe

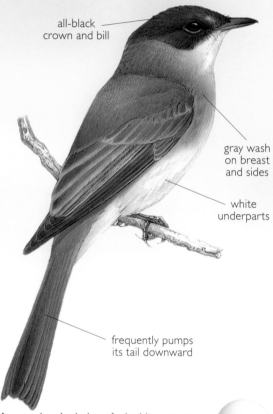

all-black
crown and bill

gray wash
on breast
and sides

white
underparts

frequently pumps
its tail downward

Nesting: under the ledge of a building, picnic shelter, bridge or in a culvert, cliff or well; cup-shaped mud nest is lined with soft material; unmarked, white eggs are ¾ x ⁹⁄₁₆ in; female incubates 4–5 eggs for about 16 days.

Did You Know?

Eastern Phoebes sometimes reuse their nest sites for many years. Females that save energy by reusing their nest are often able to lay more eggs.

Look For

Some other birds pump their tails while perched, but few species can match the zest and frequency of the Eastern Phoebe's tail pumping.

Great Crested Flycatcher

Myiarchus crinitus

Loud, raucous calls give away the presence of the brightly colored Great Crested Flycatcher. This large flycatcher often inhabits forest edges and nests in woodlands throughout Kansas. Unlike other eastern flycatchers, the Great Crested prefers to nest in a tree cavity or abandoned woodpecker hole, or sometimes uses a nest box intended for a bluebird. Occasionally, the Great Crested Flycatcher will decorate the entrance to its nest with a shed snakeskin; if none is available it may substitute translucent plastic wrap. The purpose of this practice is not fully understood, though it may serve as a warning to would-be predators.

Other ID: dark olive brown upperparts; heavy, black bill.
Size: *L* 8–9 in; *W* 13 in.
Voice: loud, whistled *wheep!* and a rolling *prrrrreet!*
Status: common summer resident.
Habitat: deciduous and mixed woodlands, usually near openings or edges; parks and neighborhoods with tall trees.

Similar Birds

Western Kingbird

Olive-sided Flycatcher

Ash-throated Flycatcher

peaked head

rufous brown wings and tail

gray throat and upper breast

bright yellow belly and undertail coverts

Nesting: in a tree cavity or artificial cavity lined with grass; may hang a shed snakeskin over entrance hole; heavily marked, pale buff eggs are ⅞ x ⅝ in; female incubates 5 eggs for 13–15 days.

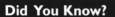

Did You Know?

Many animals and birds depend on tree cavities for shelter. A large dead tree can often be just as beneficial for birds as a living one.

Look For

Follow the loud *wheep!* calls and watch for a show of bright yellow and rufous feathers to find this flycatcher.

Western Kingbird
Tyrannus verticalis

Kingbirds perch on wires or fence posts in open
habitats and fearlessly chase larger birds from their
breeding territories. Once you have witnessed a
kingbird's brave attacks against much larger birds,
such as crows and hawks, you'll understand why
this rabble-rouser was awarded its regal common
name. • The tumbling aerial courtship display of
the Western Kingbird is a good indication that this
bird might be breeding. The male twists and turns
as he rises to heights of 65 feet above the ground,
stalls, then tumbles and flips his way back to the
earth.

Other ID: black bill; faint, dark gray mask; thin,
orange crown (rarely seen); pale gray breast; black
tail; white edges on outer tail feathers.
Size: L 8–9 in; W 15½ in.
Voice: chatty, twittering *whit-ker-whit;* also a short
kit or extended *kit-kit-keetle-dot.*
Status: common migrant and summer
resident.
Habitat: open, dry country; grassy
areas with scattered brush or hedgerows; edges of open fields; riparian
woodlands, parks and residential areas.

Similar Birds

Great Crested
Flycatcher

Cassin's Kingbird

pale gray head

ashy gray wing
coverts

whitish
throat

yellow belly and
undertail coverts

Nesting: in deciduous tree or on a utility pole;
bulky cup nest of grass and twigs is lined with
soft material; whitish, heavily blotched eggs are
⅞ x ⅝ in; female incubates 3–5 eggs 18–19 days.

Did You Know?

The scientific name *verticalis* refers to the bird's
hidden orange crown
patch, which is flared during courtship displays and
in combat with rivals.

Look For

This kingbird has been known
to capture insects flushed by
lawnmowers. When a king-
bird spots an insect, it may
chase it for up to 50 feet
before capturing it.

Eastern Kingbird
Tyrannus tyrannus

Sometimes referred to as the "Jekyll and Hyde" bird, the Eastern Kingbird is a gregarious fruit eater while wintering in South America, and an antisocial, aggressive insect eater while nesting in North America. • The Eastern Kingbird fearlessly attacks crows, hawks and even humans that pass through its territory, pursuing and pecking at them until the threat has passed. No one familiar with the Eastern Kingbird's pugnacious behavior will refute its scientific name, *Tyrannus tyrannus*. It has even been observed stealing nesting material from the bottom of oriole nests. This bird reveals a gentler side of its character in its quivering, butterfly-like courtship flight.

Other ID: black bill and legs; no eye ring; grayish breast.
Size: *L* 8½–9 in; *W* 15 in.
Voice: call is a quick, loud, chattering *kit-kit-kitter-kitter;* also a buzzy *dzee-dzee-dzee.*
Status: common migrant and summer resident.
Habitat: fields with scattered shrubs, trees or hedgerows, forest fringes, clearings, shrubby roadsides, towns and farmyards.

Similar Birds

Tree Swallow
(p. 144)

Olive-sided Flycatcher

small head crest

thin, orange-red crown
(rarely seen)

dark gray to black
upperparts

white underparts

white-tipped tail

Nesting: on a horizontal limb, stump or
upturned tree root; cup nest is made of weeds,
twigs and grass; darkly blotched, white to pinkish white eggs are 1 x ¾ in; female incubates
3–4 eggs for 14–18 days.

Did You Know?

Eastern Kingbirds rarely
walk or hop on the
ground—they prefer to
fly, even for very short
distances.

Look For

Eastern Kingbirds are common and widespread. On a
drive in the country you will
likely spot at least one of
these birds sitting on a fence
or utility wire.

Loggerhead Shrike
Lanius ludovicianus

The Loggerhead Shrike is truly in a class of its own. This predatory songbird has very acute vision. It often perches atop trees and on wires to scan for small prey, which is caught in fast, direct flight or a swooping dive. • The male displays its hunting prowess by impaling prey on thorns or barbed wire, earning it the nickname "Butcherbird." This behavior may also serve as a means of storing excess food during times of plenty. • Many shrikes are killed by traffic as they fly low across roads to prey on insects attracted to the warm pavement.

Other ID: gray crown and back; white underparts. *In flight:* white wing patches; white-edged tail.
Size: L 9 in; W 12 in.
Voice: *Male:* high-pitched, hiccupy *bird-ee bird-ee* in summer; infrequently a harsh *shack-shack* year-round.
Status: uncommon summer resident and migrant; rare in winter.
Habitat: grazed pastures and marginal and abandoned farmlands with scattered hawthorn shrubs, fence posts, barbed wire and nearby wetlands; often seen near cattle.

Similar Birds

Northern Shrike

Northern Mockingbird

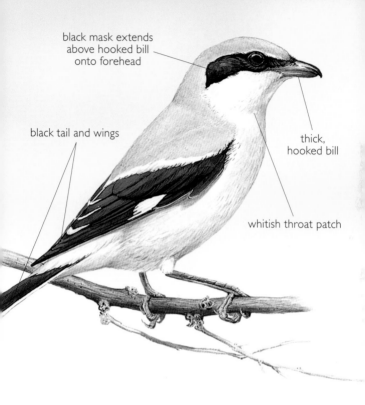

black mask extends above hooked bill onto forehead

black tail and wings

thick, hooked bill

whitish throat patch

Nesting: low in a shrub or small tree; bulky cup nest of twigs and grass is lined with animal hair, feathers and plant down; darkly blotched, pale buff to grayish white eggs are 1 x ¾ in; female incubates 5–6 eggs for 15–17 days.

Did You Know?

Habitat loss has contributed to a steady decline in Loggerhead Shrike populations, earning this bird endangered species status in parts of North America.

Look For

Shrikes typically perch at the top of tall trees to survey the surrounding area for prey.

Warbling Vireo
Vireo gilvus

The Warbling Vireo is a common summer resident across Kansas. This vireo often settles close to urban areas, and by May its bubbly voice may be heard in parks, backyards and shelterbelts. Since the Warbling Vireo lacks any splashy field marks, it is often very difficult to see as it forages high in a tree. • Vireos are larger, have a larger bill, and typically move slower than warblers. • Ten species of vireos have been seen in Kansas.

Other ID: white to pale gray underparts; brighter adults may have yellowish sides. *In flight:* broad-winged; drab above, white below.
Size: *L* 5–5½ in. W 8–9 in.
Voice: male's song is a long, musical warble of slurred whistles; cat-like calls, 2-syllabled notes and a short, dry *gwit*.
Status: common migrant and summer resident.
Habitat: deciduous forests, riparian woodlands; urban parks, orchards and shelterbelts.

Similar Birds

Red-eyed Vireo   Philadelphia Vireo   Bell's Vireo

partial gray eye line bordering white eyebrow

gray crown

olive gray upperparts

no wing bars

yellowish flanks

Nesting: in a horizontal fork of a tree or shrub; hanging basket-like cup nest of grass, roots, plant down and spider's silk; dark-spotted, white eggs are ¾ x ⁹⁄₁₆ in; pair incubates 4 eggs for 12 days.

Did You Know?

This bird breeds throughout much of North America, the broadest breeding range of our vireos.

Look For

Some Warbling Vireos are brighter with more yellow in their plumage and can be confused with the Philadelphia Vireo, an uncommon migrant through eastern Kansas.

Blue Jay

Cyanocitta cristata

The Blue Jay is a familiar sight throughout Kansas. White-flecked wing feathers and sharply defined facial features on an otherwise mostly blue body make this songbird easy to recognize. • Jays can be quite aggressive when competing for sunflower seeds and peanuts at backyard feeding stations and rarely hesitate to drive away smaller birds, squirrels or threatening cats. Even the Great Horned Owl is not too formidable a predator for a group of these brave, boisterous birds to harass.

Other ID: blue upperparts; white underparts; black bill.
Size: *L* 11–12 in; *W* 16 in.
Voice: noisy, screaming *jay-jay-jay;* nasal *queedle queedle queedle-queedle* sounds like a muted trumpet; often imitates various sounds, including calls of other birds.
Status: common permanent resident in eastern two-thirds of Kansas, uncommon in western third of the state.
Habitat: mixed deciduous forests, agricultural areas, scrubby fields and townsites.

Similar Birds

Western Scrub-Jay

Steller's Jay

Pinyon Jay

blue crest

white bars
and flecking
on the wings

black "necklace"

blue tail with dark
bars and white
corners

Nesting: in a tree or tall shrub; pair builds
a bulky stick nest; greenish, buff or pale eggs,
spotted with gray and brown, are 1⅛ x ¾ in;
pair incubates 4–5 eggs for 16–18 days.

Did You Know?

Blue Jays store food from
feeders in trees and other
places for later use.

Look For

Three species of jays from the
western U.S.—Steller's Jays,
Pinyon Jays and Western
Scrub-Jays—occasionally visit
western Kansas in winter.

Black-billed Magpie
Pica hudsonia

Truly among North America's most beautiful birds, Black-billed Magpies are too often discredited because of their aggressive demeanor. Whereas many westerners consider magpies a nuisance, eastern visitors to Kansas are often captivated by their beauty and relative tameness. • The magpie is one of the most exceptional architects among birds. The domed nest compartment conceals and protects eggs and young from harsh weather and predators. Abandoned nests remain in trees for years and are often reused by other birds. • Magpies may be declining in some areas because of West Nile virus.

Other ID: black head, breast and back; white belly; black undertail coverts. *In flight:* rounded, black and white wings.
Size: *L* 18 in; *W* 25 in.
Voice: loud, nasal, frequently repeated *ueh-ueh-ueh;* also many other vocalizations.
Status: common resident in the western half of Kansas; rare in eastern Kansas in fall and winter.
Habitat: open forests, agricultural areas, riparian thickets, townsites and campgrounds.

Look For

Albino magpies occasionally occur. Their bellies are white, just like the bellies of regular magpies, but their body feathers are light gray instead of black.

large, black bill

iridescent wings and
very long tail may
appear black

white wing
patch

Nesting: in a tree or tall shrub; domed stick
and twig nest is often held together with mud;
brown-spotted, greenish gray eggs are 1¼ x 1 in;
female incubates 5–8 eggs for up to 24 days.

Did You Know?

Magpies raised in captivity may learn how to imitate the
human voice and "count" or tell apart different-sized groups
of objects.

American Crow
Corvus brachyrhynchos

Members of the highly social Corvid family are among the most clever birds. They have superb memories and are able to learn, make simple tools and solve problems. Crows will often drop walnuts or clams from great heights onto a hard surface to crack the shells, one of the few examples of birds using objects to manipulate food. • The Fish Crow, recognized by its high nasal call, is found along rivers in southeast Kansas. The Chihuahuan Raven and rare Common Raven of western Kansas are larger with bigger bills and wedge-shaped tails. • This wary bird is also an impressive mimic, able to whine like a dog and laugh or cry like a human.

Other ID: glossy, purple-black plumage; black bill and legs.
Size: *L* 17–21 in; *W* 3 ft.
Voice: distinctive, far-carrying, repetitive *caw-caw-caw*.
Status: common year-round resident.
Habitat: urban areas, agricultural fields and other open areas with scattered woodlands.

Similar Birds

Chihuahuan Raven

Common Raven

Fish Crow

short, square-shaped tail

slim, sleek head
and throat

Nesting: in a tree or on a utility pole; large
stick-and-branch nest is lined with fur and soft
plant material; darkly blotched, gray-green to
blue-green eggs are 1⅝ x 1⅛ in; female incubates 4–6 eggs for about 18 days.

Did You Know?

Crows are family oriented,
and the young from the
previous year may help
their parents to raise the
nestlings.

Look For

Large roosts with hundreds
of crows may form in towns
during winter.

Horned Lark
Eremophila alpestris

The tinkling song of the Horned Lark is always an early sign of spring in Kansas. Long before many other birds have returned, the male Horned Lark is already performing its high-speed, plummeting courtship dive. This species has been known to remain on the nest, protecting its eggs, even during late spring blizzards. • Horned Larks are often abundant at roadsides, searching for seeds, but an approaching vehicle usually sends them flying into an adjacent field. Huge flocks gather in winter, especially in western Kansas, and these flocks usually contain longspurs.

Other ID: *Male:* light yellow to white face; pale throat; dull brown upperparts. *Female:* duller plumage.
Size: *L* 7 in; *W* 12 in.
Voice: call is a tinkling *tsee-titi* or *zoot;* flight song is a long series of tinkling, twittered whistles.
Status: common resident throughout state; abundant in winter in central and western Kansas.
Habitat: open areas, including pastures, native prairie, cultivated or sparsely vegetated fields, golf courses and airfields.

Similar Birds

Lapland Longspur
(p. 202)

American Pipit

Snow Bunting

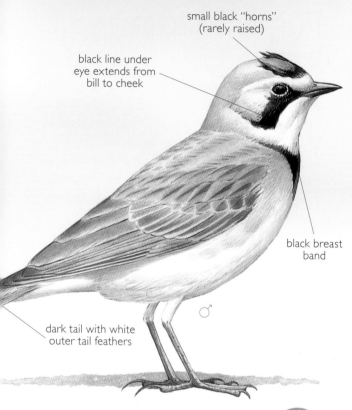

small black "horns"
(rarely raised)

black line under
eye extends from
bill to cheek

black breast
band

♂

dark tail with white
outer tail feathers

Nesting: on the ground; in a shallow scrape lined with grass, plant fibers and roots; brown-blotched, gray to greenish white eggs are 1 x ⅝ in; female incubates 3–4 eggs for 10–12 days.

Did You Know?

One way to distinguish sparrows from Horned Larks is by their method of travel: Horned Larks walk, but sparrows hop.

Look For

This bird's dark tail contrasts with its light brown body and belly. Look for this feature to identify flying Horned Larks in their open-country habitat.

Purple Martin
Progne subis

These large swallows will entertain you throughout spring and summer in return for you setting
up luxurious "condo complexes" for them. You
can watch martin adults spiral around their
accommodations in pursuit of flying insects, while
their young perch clumsily at the cavity openings.
Purple Martins once nested in natural tree hollows
and in cliff crevices but now have virtually abandoned these in favor of human-made housing.
• To avoid the invasion of aggressive House Sparrows
or European Starlings, it is essential for martin
condos to be cleaned out and closed up after each
nesting season. Open them again in early April
just in time for the returning martins.

Other ID: pointed wings; small bill.
Size: L 7–8 in; W 18 in.
Voice: rich, fluty, robinlike *pew-pew*,
often heard in flight.
Status: common migrant and summer
resident.
Habitat: semi-open areas, often near
water.

Similar Birds

European Starling
(p. 172)

Northern Rough-wing
Swallow

♀

slightly
forked tail

glossy, dark
blue body

dark
underparts

♂

Nesting: communal; in a birdhouse or a hollowed-out gourd; nest is made of feathers, grass and mud; white eggs are 1 x ⅝ in; female incubates 4–5 eggs for 15–18 days.

Did You Know?

The Purple Martin is North America's largest swallow.

Look For

During late summer before migrating south, hundreds of martins may congregate in the evening to form enormous roosts.

Tree Swallow
Tachycineta bicolor

Tree Swallows often use nest boxes, including bluebird houses. When conditions are favorable, these busy birds are known to return to their young 10 to 20 times per hour (140 to 300 times a day!). This nearly ceaseless activity provides observers with plenty of opportunities to watch and photograph these birds in action. • In the evening and during light rains, small groups of foraging Tree Swallows sail gracefully above rivers and wetlands, catching stoneflies, mayflies and caddisflies.

Other ID: white underparts; no white on cheek. *Female:* slightly duller. *Immature:* brown above; white below. *In flight:* long, pointed wings.
Size: L 5½ in; W 14½ in.
Voice: alarm call is a metallic, buzzy *klweet*. *Male:* song is a liquid, chattering twitter.
Status: common migrant; widely scattered summer resident, mostly in eastern Kansas.
Habitat: stumps of dead trees found in Kansas reservoirs, wetlands, fence-lines with bluebird nest boxes and fringes of open woodlands, especially near standing water.

Similar Birds

Northern Rough-wing
Swallow

Bank Swallow

iridescent, dark blue or blue-green head and upperparts

small bill

shallowly forked tail

Nesting: in a tree cavity or nest box lined with weeds, grass and feathers; white eggs are ¾ x ½ in; female incubates 4–6 eggs for up to 19 days.

Did You Know?

When Tree Swallows leave the nest to forage, they frequently cover their eggs with feathers from the nest.

Look For

In the bright sunshine, the back of the Tree Swallow appears blue; prior to fall migration the back appears green.

Cliff Swallow
Petrochelidon pyrrhonota

In recent decades Cliff Swallows have expanded their range across North America, nesting on various human-made structures, including bridges, culverts and under eaves. During breeding season, they are common throughout Kansas and are often seen catching insects over agricultural fields, marshes, rivers and lakes. • Master mud masons, Cliff Swallows roll mud into balls with their bills and press the pellets together to form their gourd-shaped nests. Brooding parents peer out of the circular neck of the nest, their white forehead patch warning intruders that somebody is home. • The very similar Cave Swallow has only been recorded a few times in Kansas, but it may become a more common sight in coming years.

Other ID: blue-gray wings; buff breast and rump; whitish belly. *In flight:* spotted undertail coverts; nearly square tail.
Size: L 5½ in; W 13½ in.
Voice: twittering *chatter, churrr-churrr;* also an alarm call, *nyew.*
Status: common migrant and summer resident.
Habitat: bridges, steep banks, cliffs and buildings, often near watercourses.

Similar Birds

Barn Swallow
(p. 148)

Cave Swallow

blue-gray cap

rusty cheek

sharply defined, whitish forehead patch

dark throat

blue-gray wings

Nesting: colonial; under a bridge, on a cliff or under building eaves; pair builds gourd-shaped mud nest; pale, brown-spotted eggs are ¾ x ⁹⁄₁₆ in; pair incubates 4–5 eggs for 14–16 days.

Did You Know?

Cliff Swallows drink on the wing by skimming the water's surface with their open bill.

Look For

This swallow has a square (not forked) tail, cinnamon-colored rump patch and distinctive flight pattern, ascending with rapid wing-strokes then gliding down.

Barn Swallow
Hirundo rustica

When you encounter this bird, you might first notice its distinctive, deeply forked tail—or you might just find yourself repeatedly ducking to avoid the dives of a protective parent. Barn Swallows once nested on cliffs, but they are now found more frequently nesting on barns, boathouses and under bridges and house eaves. The messy young and aggressive parents unfortunately often motivate people to remove nests just as nesting season is beginning, but this bird's close association with humans allows us to observe the normally secretive reproductive cycle of birds.
• This species is found in many parts of the world.

Other ID: blue-black upperparts; long, pointed wings.
Size: L 7 in; W 15 in.
Voice: continuous, twittering chatter: *zip-zip-zip* or *kvick-kvick*.
Status: common migrant and summer resident.
Habitat: open rural and urban areas where bridges, culverts and buildings are found near water.

Similar Birds

Cliff Swallow
(p. 146)

Look For

Barn Swallows roll mud into small balls and build their nests with one mouthful of mud at a time.

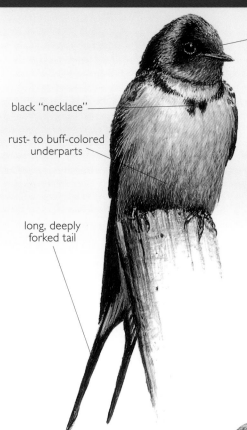

rufous throat
and forehead

black "necklace"

rust- to buff-colored
underparts

long, deeply
forked tail

Nesting: singly or in a small, loose colony; on a human-made structure under an overhang; half or full cup nest is made of mud, grass and straw; brown-spotted, white eggs are ¾ x ½ in; pair incubates 4–7 eggs for 13–17 days.

Did You Know?

The Barn Swallow is a natural pest controller, feeding on insects that are often harmful to crops and livestock. Though it is most active during the day, this swallow will feed at night in artificially lit areas.

Black-capped Chickadee
Poecile atricapillus

You can catch a glimpse of this incredibly sociable chickadee at any time of the year. In winter, Black-caps feed alongside kinglets, nuthatches, creepers and small woodpeckers; in spring and fall, they join mixed flocks of vireos and warblers. • On cold nights, chickadees enter into a hypothermic state, lowering their body temperature and heartbeat considerably to conserve energy. • The nearly identical Carolina Chickadee replaces the Black-capped Chickadee in southern Kansas. It is best identified by its four-note song and faster *chick-a-dee* call. The Mountain Chickadee is a rare winter visitor to western Kansas.

Other ID: white underparts; light buff sides and flanks; dark legs.
Size: *L* 5–6 in; *W* 8 in.
Voice: call is a chipper, whistled *chick-a-dee-dee-dee;* song is a slow, whistled *swee-tee* or *fee-bee.*
Status: common year-round resident except in southern and extreme western Kansas.
Habitat: deciduous and mixed forests, riparian woodlands, wooded urban parks; backyard feeders.

Similar Birds

Carolina Chickadee   Mountain Chickadee   Blackpoll Warbler

black cap and "bib"

white cheek

gray back
and wings

white edging on
wing feathers

Nesting: pair excavates a cavity in a rotting tree or stump; cavity is lined with fur, feathers, moss, grass and cocoons; occasionally uses a birdhouse; finely speckled, white eggs are $\frac{5}{8}$ x $\frac{1}{2}$ in; female incubates 6–8 eggs for 12–13 days.

Did You Know?

Black-capped Chickadees are thought to possess amazing memories. They can relocate a seed cache up to a month after it was hidden!

Look For

The Black-capped Chickadee sometimes feeds while hanging upside down, giving it the chance to grab a treat other birds may not be able to reach.

Tufted Titmouse
Baeolophus bicolor

This bird's amusing feeding antics and insatiable appetite keep curious observers entertained at bird feeders. Grasping a sunflower seed with its tiny feet, the dexterous Tufted Titmouse will strike its dainty bill repeatedly against the hard outer coating to expose the inner core. • A breeding pair of Tufted Titmice will maintain their bond throughout the year, even when joining small, mixed flocks for the cold winter months. The titmouse family bond is so strong that the young from one breeding season will often stay with their parents long enough to help them with nesting and feeding duties the following year.

Other ID: white underparts; pale face.
Size: *L* 6–6½ in; *W* 10 in.
Voice: noisy, scolding call; song is a whistled *peter peter* or *peter peter peter*.
Status: common year-round resident in eastern half of Kansas
Habitat: deciduous woodlands, groves and suburban parks with large, mature trees.

Similar Birds

Cedar Waxwing
(p. 174)

Bushtit

Northern Cardinal,
juvenile (p. 204)

black forehead

gray crest and upperparts

buffy flanks

Nesting: in a natural cavity or an abandoned woodpecker nest; cavity is lined with soft vegetation, moss and animal hair; brown-speckled, white eggs are $^{11}/_{16}$ x $^{9}/_{16}$ in; female incubates 5–6 eggs for 12–14 days.

Did You Know?

Nesting pairs search for soft nest lining material in late winter and may accept an offering of the hair that has accumulated in your hairbrush.

Look For

Tufted Titmice can often be seen at feeders. They always choose the largest sunflower seeds available, and during winter, they often cache food in bark crevices.

White-breasted Nuthatch
Sitta carolinensis

Its upside-down antics and noisy, nasal call make the White-breasted Nuthatch a favorite among novice birders. Whether you spot this black-capped bullet spiraling headfirst down a tree or clinging to the underside of a branch in search of invertebrates, the nuthatch's odd behavior deserves a second glance. • In migration and winter, the White-breasted Nuthatch may be joined at bird feeders by its smaller relative the Red-breasted Nuthatch, especially if pines and other conifer trees are nearby.

Other ID: white underparts and face; straight bill; short legs. *Male:* black cap. *Female:* dark gray cap.
Size: L 5½–6 in; W 11 in.
Voice: song is a fast, nasal *yank-hank yank-hank,* lower than the Red-breasted Nuthatch; calls include *ha-ha-ha ha-ha-ha, ank ank* and *ip.*
Status: common year-round resident in eastern Kansas; less common in western Kansas.
Habitat: mixed forests, woodlots and backyards.

Similar Birds

Red-breasted
Nuthatch

Brown Creeper

rusty undertail
coverts

short tail

gray-blue
back

dark crown

♀

♂

Nesting: in a natural cavity or an abandoned woodpecker nest; female lines the cavity with soft material; brown-speckled, white eggs are ¾ x ⁹⁄₁₆ in; female incubates 5–8 eggs for 12–14 days.

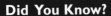

Did You Know?

Nuthatches are presumably named for their habit of wedging seeds and nuts into crevices and hacking them open with their bills.

Look For

While woodpeckers and creepers use their tails to brace themselves against tree trunks, nuthatches grasp the tree through foot power alone.

Carolina Wren
Thryothorus ludovicianus

The energetic, cheerful Carolina Wren can be shy and retiring, often hiding deep inside dense shrubbery. A nesting Carolina Wren will give intruders a severe scolding, remaining undetectable all the while. • Pairs perform lively "duets" at any time of day and in any season. The duet often begins with introductory chatter by the female, followed by ringing variations of *tea-kettle tea-kettle tea-kettle tea* from her mate. • Carolina Wrens readily nest in the brushy thickets of an overgrown backyard or in an obscure nook in a house or barn. If conditions are favorable, two broods may be raised in a single season.

Other ID: white throat; slightly downcurved bill.
Size: *L* 5½ in; *W* 7½ in.
Voice: loud, repetitious *tea-kettle tea-kettle tea-kettle* may be heard at any time of the day or year; female often chatters while male sings.
Status: common resident in eastern Kansas; rare in western Kansas.
Habitat: dense forest undergrowth, especially shrubby tangles and thickets.

Similar Birds

House Wren
(p. 158)

Winter Wren

Bewick's Wren

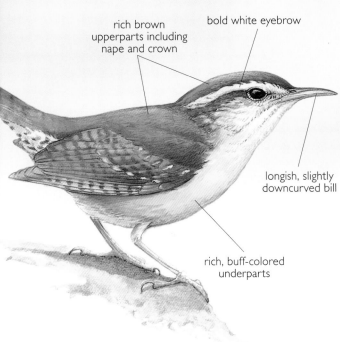

rich brown upperparts including nape and crown

bold white eyebrow

longish, slightly downcurved bill

rich, buff-colored underparts

Nesting: in a nest box or natural or artificial cavity; nest is lined with soft material and may include a snakeskin; brown-blotched, white eggs are ¾ x ⁹⁄₁₆ in; female incubates 4–5 eggs for 12–16 days.

Did You Know?

In mild winters, Carolina Wren populations remain stable or increase, but frigid winters can temporarily decimate an otherwise healthy population.

Look For

The best opportunity for viewing this particularly vocal wren is when it sits on a conspicuous perch while unleashing its impressive song.

House Wren
Troglodytes aedon

The bland, nondescript plumage of this suburban and city park dweller can be overlooked until you hear it sing a seemingly unending song in one breath. The voice of the House Wren is as sweet as that of a nightingale. • Despite its bubbly warble, this wren can be very aggressive toward other species that nest in its territory, puncturing and tossing eggs from other birds' nests. A House Wren often builds numerous nests, which later serve as decoys or "dummy" nests to fool would-be enemies.

Other ID: whitish throat; brown upperparts; whitish to buff underparts; faintly barred flanks.
Size: L 4½–5 in; W 6 in.
Voice: smooth, running, bubbly warble: *tsi-tsi-tsi-tsi oodle-oodle-oodle-oodle*.
Status: common summer resident.
Habitat: thickets and shrubby openings in or at the edge of deciduous or mixed woodlands; often in shrubs and thickets near buildings.

Similar Birds

Sedge Wren   Winter Wren   Bewick's Wren

short, upraised tail is finely barred with black

fine, dark barring on upper wings and lower back

faint buff eyebrow and eye ring

Nesting: in a natural or artificial cavity or abandoned woodpecker nest; nest of sticks and grass is lined with feathers and fur; heavily marked, white eggs are ⅝ x ½ in; female incubates 6–8 eggs for 12–15 days.

Did You Know?

This bird has the largest range of any New World passerine, stretching from Canada to southern South America.

Look For

Like all wrens, the House Wren usually carries its short tail raised upward.

Golden-crowned Kinglet

Regulus satrapa

The dainty Golden-crowned Kinglet is not much bigger than a hummingbird, and you may just barely hear its high-pitched calls as it gleans for insects, berries and sap in the forest canopy. Its small size exposes it to unique hazards, such as perishing on the burrs of burdock plants. • "Pishing" and squeaking sounds often lure these songbirds into an observable range. Behavioral traits, such as its perpetual motion and chronic wing flicking, can help identify Golden-crowns from a distance.

Other ID: black border around crown; black eye line; dark cheek; olive back; darker wings and tail; light underparts.

Size: *L* 4 in; *W* 7 in.

Voice: song is a faint, high-pitched, accelerating *tsee-tsee-tsee-tsee, why do you shilly-shally?;* call is a very high-pitched *tsee tsee tsee.*

Status: common migrant and uncommon winter resident.

Habitat: coniferous, deciduous and mixed forests; sometimes visits urban parks and gardens.

Similar Birds

Ruby-crowned Kinglet

Look For

Golden-crowns are often joined by flocks of chickadees, Red-breasted Nuthatches and Brown Creepers at the tops of pines.

reddish orange crown

white eyebrow

2 white wing bars

yellow crown

♂

♀

Nesting: usually in a spruce or other conifer; hanging nest is made of moss, lichens, twigs and leaves; pale buff eggs, spotted with gray and brown, are ½ x ⅜ in; female incubates 8–9 eggs for 14–15 days.

Did You Know?

The Golden-crowned Kinglet's scientific name, *Regulus,* is derived from the Latin word for "king," a fitting name for a bird that wears a golden crown!

Eastern Bluebird
Sialia sialis

The Eastern Bluebird's enticing colors are like those of a warm setting sun against a deep blue sky. • This cavity nester's survival has been put to the test—populations have declined in the presence of the introduced House Sparrow and European Starling, which compete with bluebirds for nest sites. The removal of standing dead trees has also diminished nest site availability. Thankfully, bluebird enthusiasts and organizations have developed "bluebird trails" and mounted nest boxes on fence posts along highways and rural roads, allowing Eastern Bluebird numbers to gradually recover.

Other ID: dark bill and legs. *Female:* thin, white eye ring; gray-brown head and back tinged with blue; blue wings and tail; paler chestnut underparts.
Size: *L* 7 in; *W* 13 in.
Voice: song is a rich, warbling *turr, turr-lee, turr-lee;* call is a chittering *pew.*
Status: common year-round resident in eastern Kansas; rare in winter in the west.
Habitat: fencelines, meadows, fallow fields, forest clearings and edges, golf courses, large lawns and cemeteries.

Similar Birds

Mountain Bluebird

Blue-gray Gnatcatcher

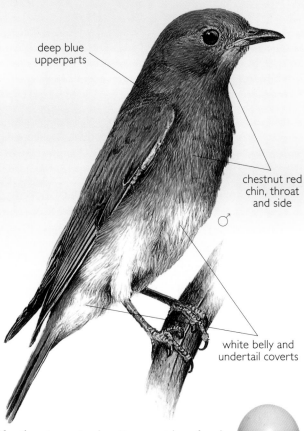

deep blue upperparts

chestnut red chin, throat and side

♂

white belly and undertail coverts

Nesting: in a natural cavity or nest box; female builds a cup nest of grass, weed stems and small twigs; pale blue eggs are ⅞ x ⅝ in; female incubates 4–5 eggs for 13–16 days.

Did You Know?

Nestlings that have fledged before they can fly and adults that are too wet to fly may be seen climbing trees.

Look For

Bluebirds have straight, pointed bills that are perfect for capturing insects. They also feed on berries and are especially attracted to wild grapes, sumac and currants.

American Robin
Turdus migratorius

Come March, the familiar song of the American Robin may wake you early if you are a light sleeper. This abundant bird adapts easily to urban areas and often works from dawn until after dusk when there is a nest to be built or hungry, young mouths to feed.
• The robin's bright red belly contrasts with its dark head and wings, making this bird easy to identify.
• American Robins do not use nest boxes; they prefer platforms for their nests. Robins usually raise two broods per year, and the male cares for the fledglings from the first brood while the female incubates the second clutch of eggs.

Other ID: incomplete, white eye ring; gray-brown back; white undertail coverts.
Size: L 10 in; W 17 in.
Voice: song is an evenly spaced warble: *cheerily cheer-up cheerio;* call is a rapid *tut-tut-tut.*
Status: abundant migrant and summer resident; sometimes common during mild winters, especially if food (such as redcedar berries) is plentiful.
Habitat: *Breeding:* residential lawns and gardens, pastures, urban parks, broken forests and river shorelines. *Winter:* near fruit-bearing trees and open water.

Similar Birds

Townsend's Solitaire

Hermit Thrush

Swainson's Thrush

black head

dark gray head

black-tipped, yellow bill

♂

♀

white throat is streaked with black

brick red breast is darker on male

Nesting: in a tree or shrub; cup nest is built of grass, moss, bark and mud; light blue eggs are 1⅛ x ¾ in; female incubates 4 eggs for 11–16 days; raises up to 3 broods per year.

Did You Know?

In winter, fruit trees may attract flocks of robins, which gather to drink the fermenting fruit's intoxicating juices.

Look For

A hunting robin with its head tilted to the side isn't listening for prey—it is actually looking for movements in the soil.

Gray Catbird

Dumetella carolinensis

The Gray Catbird is an accomplished mimic that may fool you as it shuffles through underbrush and dense riparian shrubs, calling its catlike meow. Its mimicking talents are further enhanced by its ability to sing two notes at once, using each side of its syrinx individually. • The Gray Catbird will vigilantly defend its territory against sparrows, robins, cowbirds and other intruders. It will destroy the eggs and nestlings of other songbirds and will take on an intense defensive posture if approached, screaming and even attempting to hit an intruder.

Other ID: dark gray overall; black eyes, bill and legs.
Size: L 8½–9 in; W 11 in.
Voice: calls include a catlike *meow* and a harsh *check-check*; song is a variety of warbles, squeaks and mimicked phrases interspersed with a *mew* call.
Status: common migrant and summer resident; more rare in western Kansas.
Habitat: dense thickets, brambles, shrubby or brushy areas and hedgerows, often near water.

Similar Birds

Curved-bill Thrasher

Look For

If you catch a glimpse of this bird during breeding season, watch the male raise his long slender tail into the air to show off his rust-colored undertail coverts.

black cap

long, dark gray
to black tail

rusty undertail
coverts

Nesting: in a dense shrub or thicket; bulky cup nest is made of twigs, leaves and grass; greenish blue eggs are ⅞ x ⅝ in; female incubates 4 eggs for 12–15 days.

Did You Know?

Female Brown-headed Cowbirds often lay their eggs in Gray Catbird nests, but the watchful female catbird can recognize foreign eggs and will quickly push them out of her nest.

Northern Mockingbird
Mimus polyglottos

The Northern Mockingbird has an amazing vocal repertoire that includes over 400 different song types. The male often sings incessantly throughout the breeding season, serenading into the night during a full moon. Mockingbirds can imitate almost anything, including cell phone ring tones and the "beep-beep-beep" made by industrial vehicles as they drive in reverse. In some instances, they replicate notes so accurately that even computerized sound analysis is unable to detect the difference between the original source and the mockingbird's imitation.

Other ID: gray upperparts; 2 thin, white wing bars; light gray underparts. *In flight:* large, white patch at base of black primaries.
Size: *L* 10 in; *W* 14 in.
Voice: song is a medley of mimicked phrases, often repeated 3–6 times; calls include a harsh *chair* and *chewk*.
Status: common migrant and summer resident; uncommon in winter
Habitat: hedges, suburban gardens and orchard margins with an abundance of available fruit; hedgerows of roses are especially important in winter.

Similar Birds

Loggerhead Shrike
(p. 130)

Townsend's Solitaire

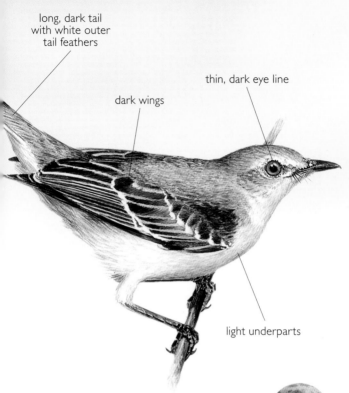

long, dark tail with white outer tail feathers

dark wings

thin, dark eye line

light underparts

Nesting: in a small shrub or tree; cup nest is built with twigs and lined with grass and leaves; brown-blotched, bluish gray to greenish eggs are 1 x ⅝ in; female incubates 3–4 eggs for 12–13 days.

Did You Know?

The scientific name *polyglottos* is Greek for "many tongues" and refers to this bird's ability to mimic a wide variety of sounds.

Look For

The Northern Mockingbird's energetic territorial dance is delightful to watch, as males square off in what appears to be a swordless fencing duel.

Brown Thrasher
Toxostoma rufum

The Brown Thrasher shares the streaked breast of a thrush and the long tail of a catbird, but it has a temper all its own. Because it nests close to the ground, the Brown Thrasher defends its nest with a vengeance, attacking snakes and other nest robbers, sometimes to the point of drawing blood. • Biologists have estimated that the male Brown Thrasher is capable of producing up to 3000 distinctive song phrases—the most extensive vocal repertoire of any North American bird. • This bird is most abundant in the central Great Plains.

Other ID: reddish brown upperparts; long, rufous tail; orange-yellow eyes.
Size: L 11½ in; W 13 in.
Voice: sings a large variety of phrases, with each phrase usually repeated twice: *dig-it dig-it, hoe-it hoe-it, pull-it-up pull-it-up;* calls include a loud crackling note, a harsh shuck, a soft churr or a whistled, 3-note *pit-cher-ee.*
Status: common migrant and summer resident.
Habitat: dense shrubs and thickets, overgrown pastures, woodland edges and brushy areas; often found in residential areas.

Similar Birds

Hermit Thrush

Wood Thrush

Curve-billed Thrasher

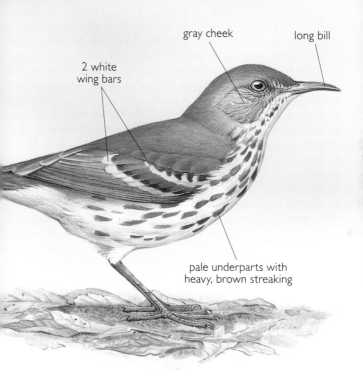

gray cheek

long bill

2 white
wing bars

pale underparts with
heavy, brown streaking

Nesting: usually in a low shrub; often on the
ground; cup nest is made of grass, twigs and
leaves; pale blue eggs, dotted with reddish
brown, are 1 x ¾ in; pair incubates 4 eggs for
11–14 days.

Did You Know?

Fencing shrubby, wooded
areas bordering wetlands
and streams can prevent
cattle from devastating
thrasher nesting habitat.

Look For

You might catch only a flash
of rufous as the Brown
Thrasher flies from one
thicket to another in its
shrubby understory habitat.

European Starling
Sturnus vulgaris

The European Starling did not hesitate to make itself known across North America after being released in New York's Central Park in 1890 and 1891. These highly adaptable birds not only took over the nesting sites of native cavity nesters, such as bluebirds and woodpeckers, but they learned to mimic the sounds of Killdeers, Red-tailed Hawks, Northern Bobwhites and meadowlarks. • Look for these birds in huge flocks around feedlots or in enormous evening roosts under bridges or on buildings. • European Starlings have a variable diet consisting of Japanese beetles and other destructive agricultural pests, berries, grains and even human food waste.

Other ID: dark eyes; iridescent black breast; short, squared tail. *Nonbreeding:* feather tips are heavily spotted with white and buff.
Size: L 8½ in; W 16 in.
Voice: variety of whistles, squeaks and gurgles; imitates other birds.
Status: abundant year-round resident.
Habitat: agricultural areas, towns, woodland edges, landfills and roadsides.

Similar Birds

Rusty Blackbird   Brewer's Blackbird

iridescent, purple-black
head, neck and breast

glossy, green back
with buffy spots

yellow bill

greenish black
underparts

Nesting: in an abandoned woodpecker cavity, natural cavity or nest box; nest is made of grass, twigs and straw; bluish to greenish white eggs are 1⅛ x ⅞ in; female incubates 4–6 eggs for 12–14 days.

Did You Know?

This bird was brought to New York as part of a Shakespeare society's plan to introduce all the birds mentioned in their favorite author's writings.

Look For

The European Starling looks somewhat like a blackbird. Look for the starling's comparably shorter tail and bright yellow bill to help you identify it.

Cedar Waxwing
Bombycilla cedrorum

With its black mask and slick hairdo, the Cedar Waxwing has a heroic look. This bird's splendid personality is reflected in its amusing antics after it gorges on fermented berries and in its gentle courtship dance. To court a mate, the gentlemanly male hops toward a female and offers her a berry. The female accepts the berry and hops away, then stops and hops back toward the male to offer him the berry in return. • If a bird's crop is full and it is unable to eat any more, it will continue to pluck fruit and pass it down the line, like a bucket brigade, until the fruit is gulped down by a still-hungry bird.

Other ID: brown upperparts; yellow terminal tail band.
Size: *L* 7 in; *W* 12 in.
Voice: faint, high-pitched, trilled whistle: *tseee-tseee-tseee.*
Status: common migrant and winter resident throughout Kansas; uncommon breeding bird in eastern Kansas.
Habitat: wooded residential parks and gardens, overgrown fields, forest edges, second-growth, riparian and open woodlands; often near fruit trees and water.

Similar Birds

Bohemian Waxwing

Look For

Waxwings will show definite signs of tipsiness after consuming fermented fruit.

cinnamon crest

black mask

small, red "drops" on wings

yellow wash on belly

yellow terminal tail band

Nesting: in a tree or shrub; cup nest is made of twigs, moss and lichen; darkly spotted, bluish to gray eggs are ⅞ x ⅝ in; female incubates 3–5 eggs for 12–16 days.

Did You Know?

The Bohemian Waxwing is a rare winter visitor in Kansas. It is larger, grayer, and it has yellow in the wings and rufous undertail coverts.

Orange-crowned Warbler
Vermivora celata

The nondescript Orange-crowned Warbler causes identification problems for many birders. Its drab, olive yellow appearance and lack of field marks makes it frustratingly similar to females of other warbler species, and the male's orange crown patch is seldom visible. • This small warbler has rather deliberate foraging movements and is usually seen gleaning insects from the leaves and buds of low shrubs. It occasionally eats berries and fruit or visits suet feeders in winter.

Other ID: variable plumage; male's orange crown patch usually hidden. *In flight:* dull olive gray wings and tail.
Size: *L* 5 in; *W* 7 in.
Voice: call is a clear, sharp *chip*.
Status: common migrant, more common in western Kansas; rare in winter.
Habitat: any wooded habitat or areas with tall shrubs.

Similar Birds

Tennessee Warbler

Nashville Warbler

Warbling Vireo
(p. 132)

greenish gray upperparts

faint, pale eyebrow

dark eye line
divides pale
eye ring

♂

♀

yellow undertail
coverts

Nesting: does not breed in Kansas; breeds in
the Arctic; on the ground or occasionally in a
low shrub; well-hidden, small cup nest is made
of grasses; darkly marked, white eggs are ⅝ x ½ in;
female incubates 4–6 eggs for 12–14 days.

Did You Know?

Vermivora is Latin for
"worm-eating" and *celata*
is derived from the Latin
word for "hidden," a reference to this bird's inconspicuous crown patch.

Look For

Orange-crowned Warblers
routinely feed on sap or
insects attracted to the sap
wells drilled by Yellow-bellied
Sapsuckers.

Yellow Warbler
Dendroica petechia

The Yellow Warbler is often parasitized by the Brown-headed Cowbird and can recognize cowbird eggs, but rather than tossing them out, this warbler will build another nest overtop the old eggs or abandon the nest completely. Occasionally, cowbirds strike repeatedly—a five-story nest was once found! • The widely distributed Yellow Warbler arrives in May, flitting from branch to branch in search of juicy caterpillars, aphids and beetles and singing its *sweet-sweet* song.

Other ID: bright yellow body; yellowish legs; black bill and eyes. *Female:* may have faint, red breast streaks.
Size: *L* 5 in; *W* 8 in.
Voice: song is a fast, frequently repeated *sweet-sweet-sweet summer sweet.*
Status: common migrant; uncommon breeding species.
Habitat: habitat generalist; moist, open woodlands, dense scrub, scrubby meadows, second-growth woodlands, riparian woods and urban parks and gardens.

Similar Birds

Wilson's Warbler

Prothonotary Warbler

beady,
dark eyes

♀

♂

red breast streaks

olive wings and
tail with bright
yellow barring

Nesting: in a deciduous tree or shrub; female builds a cup nest of grass, weeds and shredded bark; darkly speckled, greenish white eggs are ⅝ x ½ in; female incubates eggs for 11–12 days.

Did You Know?

The Yellow Warbler has an amazing geographical range. It is found throughout North America and on islands in Central and South America.

Look For

These widespread habitat generalists favor moist habitats and brushy thickets for breeding but may visit orchards and gardens during migration.

Yellow-rumped Warbler

Dendroica coronata

Yellow-rumped Warblers are the most abundant and widespread wood-warblers in North America. Apple, juniper and sumac trees laden with fruit attract these birds in winter. • This species comes in two forms: the white-throated "Myrtle Warbler" of the East, and the yellow-throated "Audubon's Warbler" of the West. The Myrtle form is commonly found throughout Kansas, whereas the Audubon's form is typically found only in extreme western Kansas.

Other ID: *"Myrtle Warbler":* thin, white eye line; two white wing bars. *Breeding male:* black cheek and breast band. *Breeding female:* gray-brown upperparts; faint brown breast streaks; fainter yellow patches. *In flight:* white corners in the tail.
Size: *L* 5½ in; *W* 9¼ in.
Voice: male's song is a brief, bubbling warble rising or falling at the end; much variation between races and individuals; call is a sharp *chip* or *chet*.
Status: abundant migrant; uncommon winter resident
Habitat: a variety of well-vegetated habitats in lowlands, especially in wax myrtle thickets.

Similar Birds

Yellow-throated Warbler

Palm Warbler

Magnolia Warbler

yellow shoulder

yellow crown

blue-gray upper-
parts with black
streaking

♂

♀

white
chin and
throat

"Myrtle Warbler"

bright yellow
rump

Nesting: does not nest in Kansas; nests in the western and northern U.S. and in Canada; in a crotch or on a horizontal limb in a conifer; cup nest is made of vegetation and spider silk; brown-blotched, buff-colored eggs are ⅝ x ½ in; female incubates 4–5 eggs for up to 13 days.

Did You Know?

This small warbler's habit of flitting near buildings to snatch spiders from their webs has earned it the nickname "spider bird."

Look For

Small puddles that form during or after rains often attract warblers, allowing a glimpse of these secretive birds.

Common Yellowthroat

Geothlypis trichas

The bumblebee colors of the male Common Yellowthroat's black mask and yellow throat identify this skulking wetland resident. He sings his *witchety* song from strategically chosen cattail perches that he visits in rotation, fiercely guarding his territory against the intrusion of other males.
• The Common Yellowthroat is different from most wood-warblers, preferring marshlands and wet, overgrown meadows to forests. The female has no mask and remains mostly hidden from view in thick vegetation when she tends to the nest.

Other ID: black bill; orangy legs. *Female:* may show faint, white eye ring.
Size: *L* 5 in; *W* 7 in.
Voice: song is a clear, oscillating *witchety witchety witchety-witch;* call is a sharp *tcheck* or *tchet.*
Status: common migrant and summer resident.
Habitat: wetlands, riparian areas and wet, overgrown meadows; sometimes dry fields.

Similar Birds

Kentucky Warbler   Hooded Warbler

olive green to olive brown upperparts

dingy white belly

♀

broad, black mask with white upper border

yellow throat and breast

♂

Nesting: on or near the ground; often in a small shrub or emergent vegetation; female builds an open cup nest of weeds, grass, bark strips and moss; brown-blotched, white eggs are ⅝ x ½ in; female incubates 3–5 eggs for 12 days.

Did You Know?

Famous Swedish biologist Carolus Linnaeus named the Common Yellowthroat in 1766, making it one of the first North American birds to be described.

Look For

Common Yellowthroats immerse themselves or roll in water, then shake off the excess water by flicking or flapping their wings.

Summer Tanager
Piranga rubra

The Summer Tanager is a treat for Kansas birders. This striking bird breeds throughout our forested areas, favoring the edges of forests and riparian areas. • Summer Tanagers thrive on a wide variety of insects but are best known for snatching flying bees and wasps from menacing swarms. They may even harass the occupants of a wasp nest until the nest is abandoned and the larvae inside are left free for the picking. • The Scarlet Tanager has black wings and is more restricted to the eastern forests, whereas the colorful Western Tanager is only found in extreme western Kansas.

Other ID: immature male has patchy, red and greenish plumage.
Size: L 7–8 in; W 12 in.
Voice: song is a series of 3–5 sweet, clear, whistled phrases, like a faster version of the American Robin's song; call is *pit* or *pit-a-tuck*.
Status: uncommon migrant and summer resident in eastern and central Kansas; rare migrant in western Kansas.
Habitat: mixed coniferous and decid-uous woodlands, especially those with oak or hickory, or riparian woodlands with cottonwoods; occasionally in wooded backyards.

Similar Birds

Scarlet Tanager

Western Tanager

varies from overall grayish yellow to greenish with reddish wash

small crest

thick, pale bill

♀

rose red overall

♂

Nesting: constructed on a high, horizontal tree limb; female builds a flimsy, shallow cup of grass and twigs and lines it with fine grass; pale blue-green eggs, spotted with reddish brown are ⅞ x ⅝ in; female incubates 3–4 eggs for 11–12 days.

Did You Know?

The male Summer Tanager keeps his rosy red plumage all year, unlike the male Scarlet Tanager, which temporarily molts to a greenish yellow plumage in fall.

Look For

A courting male tanager will hop persistently in front of or over the female while offering her food and fanning his handsome crest and tail feathers.

Spotted Towhee
Pipilo maculatus

Do not be disappointed if the raccoon you were expecting to see at close range turns out to be a bird slightly smaller than a robin. The Spotted Towhee is capable of quite a ruckus when it forages in loose leaf litter, scraping with both feet.

• Although they are confident birds, not hesitant to scold even the family cat, Spotted Towhees can be shy. They need some coaxing if you want to lure them into the open and they tend to make themselves scarce in parks crowded with people. If dense vegetation is nearby, they can be found feeding on the ground beneath bird feeders during winter.

Other ID: white spotting on wings and back; white outer tail corners; white breast and belly; buffy undertail. *Female:* paler overall.
Size: *L* 7–8 in; *W* 10–10½ in.
Voice: song is *here here here PLEASE;* distinctive call is a buzzy trill.
Status: common migrant and uncommon winter resident throughout Kansas; rare nesting species mostly in riparian woodlands in northern and western Kansas.
Habitat: brushy hedgerows and woods with dense understory; overgrown bushy fields and hillsides.

Similar Birds

Eastern Towhee

Black-headed
Grosbeak

Dark-eyed Junco
(p. 200)

black hood, back, wings and tail

red eyes

♂

dark, conical bill

dark rufous sides and flanks

Nesting: low in a shrub or in a depression on the ground; cup of leaves, bark and rootlets is lined with fine grasses and hair; brown-wreathed, white eggs are 1 x ¾ in; pair incubates 3–4 eggs for 12–13 days.

Did You Know?

Until recently, the Spotted Towhee was grouped with the Eastern Towhee as a single species, the "Rufous-sided Towhee."

Look For

Towhees like tangled thickets and overgrown gardens with blackberries and other small fruits as well as mature woodlands with a blanket of leaf litter on the forest floor.

American Tree Sparrow

Spizella arborea

Although its name suggests a close relationship with trees or forests, the American Tree Sparrow is actually a bird of treeless fields and semi-open, shrubby habitats. It breeds at or above the treeline at northern latitudes, then returns to the weedy fields of southern Canada and the central U.S. to overwinter. • Kansas has large numbers of these birds in late fall and winter, but most quickly head back north at the first signs of spring.

Other ID: mottled brown upperparts; notched tail; dark legs; dark face; dark upper mandible; yellow lower mandible. *Nonbreeding:* gray central crown stripe. *Juvenile:* streaky breast and head.
Size: L 6¼ in; W 9½ in.
Voice: a high, whistled *tseet-tseet* is followed by a short, sweet, musical series of slurred whistles; call is a 3-note *tsee-dle-eat*.
Status: abundant winter resident.
Habitat: brushy thickets, roadside shrubs, semi-open fields and agricultural croplands.

Similar Birds

Swamp Sparrow

Field Sparrow

Chipping Sparrow
(p. 190)

pale rufous cap

rufous stripe
behind the eye

dark, central
breast spot

2 white wing bars

gray, unstreaked
underparts

breeding

Nesting: does not nest in Kansas; nests in northern Canada and Alaska; on the ground or in a shrub; open cup nest of grass, moss, bark shreds and twigs is lined with feathers and fine grass; brown spotted, pale greenish or bluish eggs are ⅞ x ½ in; female incubates 4–6 eggs for 11–13 days.

Did You Know?

These birds begin courtship in late winter and during spring migration, singing bubbly, bright songs as they move northward.

Look For

These sparrows forage by scratching at the ground for seeds and are often seen in mixed flocks with Dark-eyed Juncos.

Chipping Sparrow
Spizella passerina

Though you may spot the relatively tame Chipping Sparrow singing from a high perch, it commonly nests at eye level, so you can easily watch its breeding and nest-building rituals. You can even take part in the building of this bird's nest by leaving samples of your pet's hair—or your own—around your backyard. • This bird's song is very similar to that of the Dark-eyed Junco. Listen for a slightly faster, drier and less musical series of notes to identify the Chipping Sparrow.

Other ID: *Breeding:* mottled brown upperparts; light gray, unstreaked underparts; dark bill. *Nonbreeding:* paler crown with dark streaks; brown eyebrow and cheek; pale lower mandible.
Size: *L* 5–6 in; *W* 8½ in.
Voice: song is a rapid, dry trill of *chip* notes; call is a high-pitched *chip*.
Status: common migrant throughout the state; uncommon nesting species, mostly in eastern Kansas.
Habitat: open areas or woodland edges; yards, gardens, cemeteries, golf courses and parks with tree and shrub borders; especially fond of conifers.

Similar Birds

Field Sparrow   Clay-colored Sparrow   American Tree
Sparrow (p. 188)

prominent rufous cap

white eyebrow

black eye line

white wing bars

breeding

Nesting: usually at mid-level in a coniferous tree; female builds a cup nest of grass and root-lets lined with hair; pale blue eggs are ¾ x ½ in; female incubates 4 eggs for 11–12 days.

Did You Know?

The Chipping Sparrow is the most common and widely distributed migrating sparrow in North America.

Look For

Chipping Sparrows forage on lawns for the seeds of grasses, dandelions and clovers. In winter, they are replaced at backyard bird feeders by the American Tree Sparrow.

Grasshopper Sparrow
Ammodramus savannarum

The Grasshopper Sparrow is named for its buzzy, insectlike song. Unique among sparrows, the male sings two completely different courtship songs: one ends in a short trill and the other is a prolonged series of high trills that vary in pitch and speed.
• These open-country birds have the best chance of nesting successfully in pastureland, fallow fields or abandon fields. Nests located along roadsides or in agricultural lands are often destroyed by mowing or early harvesting.

Other ID: flattened head profile; black eyes; unstreaked, light underparts with buff wash on breast, sides and flanks; sharp tail; may show small yellow patch on edge of forewing.
Size: L 5–5½ in; W 7½ in.
Voice: song is a high, faint, buzzy trill preceded by 1–3 high, thin whistled notes: *tea-tea-tea zeeeeeeeeee.*
Status: common summer resident.
Habitat: grasslands and grassy fields with little or no shrub or tree cover.

Similar Birds

Le Conte's Sparrow

Savannah Sparrow

Henslow's Sparrow

small, dark spot on buff cheek

dark crown with pale central stripe

mottled brown and rufous upperparts

pale eye ring

pale legs

Nesting: nests on ground in tall grass; small cup nest of grass is lined with finer material; white eggs with reddish brown specks are ¾ x ⁹⁄₁₆ in; female incubates 4–5 eggs for 11–13 days.

Did You Know?

Populations of this species are declining all over North America but seem to be relatively stable in Kansas.

Look For

This tiny sparrow is commonly seen in summer on roadside fences in many parts of rural Kansas.

Song Sparrow
Melospiza melodia

The well-named Song Sparrow is among the great singers of the bird world. By the time a young male Song Sparrow is a few months old, he has already created a courtship tune of his own, having learned the basics of melody and rhythm from his father and rival males. • In winter, adaptable Song Sparrows are common throughout Kansas and inhabit woodland edges, weedy ditches and riparian thickets. They regularly visit backyard feeders, belting out their sweet, three-part song throughout the year.

Other ID: mottled brown upperparts; rounded tail tip.
Size: *L* 6–7 in; *W* 8 in.
Voice: song is 1–4 introductory notes, such as *sweet sweet sweet,* followed by buzzy *towee,* then a short, descending trill; call is short *tsip* or *tchep.*
Status: common migrant and winter resident throughout Kansas; rare nesting species in northeastern Kansas.
Habitat: willow shrub lands, riparian thickets, forest openings and pastures, often near water.

Similar Birds

Fox Sparrow

Savannah Sparrow

Lincoln's Sparrow

brown line
behind eye

dark crown with
pale central stripe

grayish face

heavy brown streaks
converge at central
breast spot

Nesting: usually on the ground or in a low
shrub; female builds an open cup nest of grass,
weeds and bark strips; brown-blotched, greenish white eggs are ⅞ x ⅝ in; female incubates
3–5 eggs for 12–14 days.

Did You Know?

Though female songbirds
are not usually vocal, the
female Song Sparrow will
occasionally sing a tune of
her own.

Look For

The Song Sparrow pumps its
long, rounded tail in flight. It
also often issues a high-
pitched *seet* flight call.

Harris's Sparrow
Zonotrichia querula

Wintering Harris's Sparrows are very attractive with warm, brown or cinnamon-buff faces and variable amounts of black on the throat and upper breast. The size of the black "bib" is controlled by hormones and tends to increase with age, so older males are often the darkest. While "bib" size does not determine rank, body size does, and larger males regularly exert their dominance at roosting and feeding sites. • The scientific name *querula* means "plaintive" in Latin and refers to this bird's quavering, whistled song.

Other ID: *Breeding:* black crown, ear patch, throat and "bib"; gray face; black streaks on sides and flanks; white wing bars.
Size: L 7–7½ in; W 10½ in.
Voice: *jeenk* or *zheenk* call; flocks in flight give a rolling *chug-up chug-up*. *Male:* song, given mainly on breeding territory, is a series of 2–4 long, quavering whistles
Status: common to abundant migrant and winter resident.
Habitat: brushy roadsides, shrubby vegetation, forest edges and riparian thickets.

Similar Birds

House Sparrow, male
(p. 228)

Look For

Harris's Sparrows are one of the largest sparrows in North America. In winter, they often are seen feeding on spilled seeds beneath bird feeders.

white flecks on
black crown

pink-orange bill

brown face

mottled brown and
black upperparts

white underparts

brownish sides
and flanks

nonbreeding

Nesting: does not nest in Kansas; nests in the Canadian Arctic; on or near the ground, under a sheltering shrub; open cup nest of twigs and plant material; brown-marked, pale green eggs are ⅞ x ⅝ in; female incubates 3–5 eggs over 12–15 days.

Did You Know?

The first nest and eggs of this sparrow were not discovered until 1931, 97 years after the species was first described. The nest with four eggs was found near Churchill, Manitoba, by famous ornithologist George M. Sutton.

White-crowned Sparrow
Zonotrichia leucophrys

In winter, large, bold and smartly patterned White-crowned Sparrows brighten brushy hedgerows, overgrown fields and riparian areas. During migration, these sparrows may visit bird feeders stocked with cracked corn. • Research into this much-studied sparrow has given science tremendous insight into bird physiology, homing behavior and the geographic variability of song dialects. • The word *Zonotrichia* is Greek for "band" and "hair," a reference to the White-crowned Sparrow's head pattern.

Other ID: streaked brown back. *Immature:* head stripes are brown and gray, not black and white.
Size: L 5½–7 in; W 9½ in.
Voice: several dialects have been identified; song is highly variable, frequent *I-I-I-got-to-go-wee-wee-now!*; call is hard *pink* or high *seep*.
Status: common migrant and winter resident; more common in western Kansas.
Habitat: woodlots, parkland edges, brushy tangles, riparian thickets; also open, weedy fields, lawns and roadsides.

Similar Birds

White-throated
Sparrow

Look For

During migration, flocks of these sparrows flit between shrubs, picking seeds from leaf litter and sounding their surprisingly loud, high-pitched *seep* notes.

bold, black and white head stripes

orange-pink bill

gray face

2 white wing bars

gray, unstreaked underparts

Nesting: in a shrub, small conifer or on the ground; neat cup nest of vegetation is lined with fine materials; darkly marked, blue green eggs are ⅞ x ⅝ in; female incubates 3–5 eggs 11–14 days.

Did You Know?

This bird has a widespread distribution in North America, and populations in different parts of its range have different song dialects and vary significantly in behavior and in migratory and nesting habits.

Dark-eyed Junco

Junco hyemalis

Juncos usually congregate in backyards with bird feeders and sheltering conifers. These birds spend most of their time on the ground, snatching up seeds underneath bird feeders, and they

"Oregon Junco"

are readily flushed from wooded trails. • Five closely related Dark-eyed Junco subspecies live in North America. They share similar habits but differ in coloration and range. The "Slate-colored" race is common everywhere, while the dark hooded "Oregon" race occurs throughout the state, but is more common in western Kansas. The "White-winged," "Pink-sided" and "Gray-headed" races are rare winter visitors.

Other ID: *Female:* gray-brown where male is slate gray.
Size: L 6–7 in; W 9 in.
Voice: song is a long, dry trill; call is a smacking *chip* note, often given in series.
Status: common migrant and winter resident.
Habitat: shrubby woodland borders, backyard feeders.

Similar Birds

Eastern Towhee

Lark Bunting, male

Black-headed
Grosbeak

pale pink bill

dark slate gray overall

white belly and undertail coverts

white outer tail feathers

"Slate-colored Junco"

Nesting: does not breed in Kansas; breeds in northeastern U.S., western U.S., Alaska and Canada; on the ground, usually concealed; female builds a cup nest of twigs, grass, bark shreds and moss; brown-marked, whitish to bluish eggs are ¾ x ½ in; female incubates 3–5 eggs for 12–13 days.

Did You Know?

The junco is often called the "Snow Bird," and the species name, *hyemalis,* means "winter" in Greek.

Look For

This bird will flash its distinctive white outer tail feathers as it rushes for cover after being flushed.

Lapland Longspur
Calcarius lapponicus

In fall, Lapland Longspurs arrive from their breeding grounds looking like mottled, brownish sparrows. Large flocks typically appear wherever open fields offer an abundance of seeds or waste grain. Longspurs can be surprisingly inconspicuous until they are closely approached—then flocks suddenly erupt into the sky, flashing their white outer tail feathers. • On the Great Plains, longspurs often burrow beneath the snow during blizzards, emerging the following morning to feed.

Other ID: white throat and black "whisker"; white outer tail feathers. *Breeding male:* black crown, face and "bib"; chestnut nape; broad, white stripe curving down to shoulder from eye (may be tinged with buff behind eye); lightly streaked flanks. *Female:* similar to nonbreeding male but appears washed out; narrow, lightly streaked, buff breast band.
Size: L 6½ in; W 11½ in.
Voice: flight calls include a rattled *tri-di-dit* and a descending *teew*.
Status: abundant migrant and winter resident in western Kansas; uncommon migrant and winter resident in eastern third of the state.

Similar Birds

Chestnut-collared
Longspur

McCown's Longspur

Smith's Longspur

breeding

mostly gray
underwings

mottled brown
and black
upperparts

♀

faint chestnut
on nape

chestnut wing
patch

♂

nonbreeding

Habitat: pastures and croplands.
Nesting: does not nest in Kansas; nests in the
Arctic on open, hummocky tundra; ground nest
of grass and sedges is lined with finer material;
darkly marked, pale greenish, buff or grayish
eggs are ¾ x ⁹⁄₁₆ in; female incubates 4–6 eggs
for about 12 days.

Did You Know?

The Lapland Longspur
breeds in northern polar
regions, including the area
of northern Scandinavia
known as Lapland.

Look For

Some of the largest concen-
trations of Lapland Longspurs
ever recorded have been in
western Kansas. Flocks
occasionally contain millions
of individuals.

Northern Cardinal
Cardinalis cardinalis

A male Northern Cardinal will display his unforgettable, vibrant red head crest and raise his tail when he is excited or agitated. The male will vigorously defend his territory, even attacking his own reflection in a window or hubcap! • Cardinals are one of only a few bird species to maintain strong pair bonds. Some couples sing to each other year-round, while others join loose flocks, reestablishing pair bonds in spring during a "courtship feeding." A male offers a seed to the female, which she then accepts and eats.

Other ID: *Male:* red overall. *Female:* brownish buff overall; fainter mask; red crest, wings and tail.
Size: *L* 8–9 in; *W* 12 in.
Voice: call is a metallic chip; song is series of clear, bubbly whistled notes: *What cheer! What cheer! birdie-birdie-birdie what cheer!*
Status: uncommon resident in the west; common year-round resident in eastern Kansas.
Habitat: brushy thickets and shrubby tangles along forest and woodland edges; backyards and urban and suburban parks.

Similar Birds

Summer Tanager
(p. 184)

Scarlet Tanager

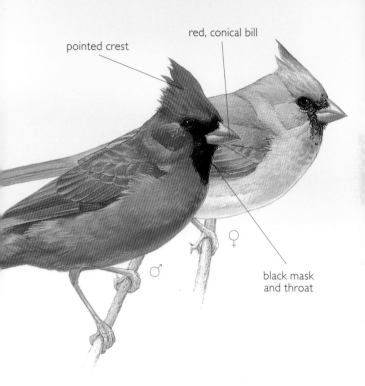

pointed crest

red, conical bill

♀

♂

black mask
and throat

Nesting: in a dense shrub or vine tangle or low
in a coniferous tree; female builds an open cup
nest of twigs, grass and bark shreds; brown-
speckled, white to greenish eggs are 1 x ¾ in;
female incubates 3–4 eggs for 12–13 days.

Did You Know?

This bird owes its name
to the vivid red plumage
of the male, which resem-
bles the robes of Roman
Catholic cardinals.

Look For

Northern Cardinals fly with
jerky movements and short
glides and have a preference
for sunflower seeds.

Indigo Bunting

Passerina cyanea

The vivid electric blue male Indigo Bunting is one of the most spectacular birds in Kansas. These birds arrive in April or May and favor raspberry thickets as nest sites. Dense, thorny stems keep most predators at a distance and the berries are a good food source. • The male is a persistent singer, vocalizing even through the heat of a summer day. A young male doesn't learn his couplet song from his parents but from neighboring males during his first year on his own. • Planting coneflowers, cosmos or foxtail grasses may attract Indigo Buntings to your backyard.

Other ID: black eyes; black legs; no wing bars. *Male:* bright blue overall; black lores. *Female:* soft brown overall; whitish throat.
Size: L 5½ in; W 8 in.
Voice: song consists of paired warbled whistles: *fire-fire, where-where, here-here, see-it see-it;* call is a quick *spit.*
Status: common summer resident.
Habitat: deciduous forest and woodland edges, regenerating forest clearings, orchards and shrubby fields.

Similar Birds

Blue Grosbeak

Mountain Bluebird

dark blue head

gray, conical bill

♂

♀

wings and tail
may show
some brown

faint brown
streaks on breast

Nesting: in a small tree, shrub or within a vine tangle; female builds a cup nest of grass, leaves and bark strips; unmarked, white to bluish white eggs are ¾ x ½ in; female incubates 3–4 eggs for 12–13 days.

Did You Know?

Females choose the most melodious males as mates, because these males can usually establish territories with the finest habitat.

Look For

The Indigo Bunting will land midway on a stem of grass or a weed and shuffle slowly toward the seed head, bending down the stem to reach the seeds.

Painted Bunting
Passerina ciris

Stunningly colorful male Painted Buntings grace Kansas thickets with their sweet songs. Although not nearly as unmistakable as adult males, the female's plumage is still attractive: a rich greenish above and pale yellow below. These birds tend to be rather secretive on their breeding grounds, often hiding in dense foliage and making observation difficult. • Painted Buntings have two separate breeding ranges: a larger, mainly inland range from Kansas and Missouri to northern Mexico, and a smaller strip along the Atlantic Coast from North Carolina to Florida.

Other ID: *Adult Female:* yellow-green above and pale yellow below; yellow orbital ring. *Juveniles:* similar to females but duller, more grayish green.
Size: L 5½ in; W 8¾ in.
Voice: song is a sweet, clear series of warbling notes; call is a sharp *chip*.
Status: common summer resident in southeastern Kansas and along the southern tier of counties west to Meade County; less common as you move westward and northward; breeds locally as far north as the slopes around Clinton and Tuttle Creek Reservoirs.
Habitat: breeds in shrubby fields.

Similar Birds

Indigo Bunting, female
(p. 206)

Blue Grosbeak, female

greenish yellow
back and wings

brilliant blue head with
red orbital ring

wholly red under-
parts including
throat

Nesting: in a shrub or low tree; female weaves
an open cup from grass, weed stems and leaves,
and lines with fine plant material and animal
hair; finely speckled, white eggs are ¾ x ⁹⁄₁₆ in;
female incubates 3–4 eggs for 11–12 days;
usually raises 2 broods per year.

Did You Know?

A breeding male, who may
have multiple mates, often
finds himself caught in
violent altercations over
territory and breeding
privileges.

Look For

Unlike some other finches,
adult male Painted Buntings
retain their bright colors during winter, which is spent in
Central and South America.

Dickcissel
Spiza americana

These "miniature meadowlarks" are a semi-nomadic, irruptive species that may be present one year in a particular location and absent the next. However, Dickcissels are generally one of the most abundant summer birds of the Kansas country-side. • Seeds and grain form the main part of their diet on their South American wintering grounds, making them unpopular with local farmers. Each year large numbers of roosting birds are poisoned in efforts to reduce crop losses, which may partially explain the Dickcissel's pattern of absence and abundance. Since winter flocks may contain over one million birds, targeting a single roost can significantly affect the world population.

Other ID: dark, conical bill; brown upperparts; pale, gray-ish underparts. *Female:* duller version of male; white throat.
Size: *L* 6–7 in; *W* 9½ in.
Voice: song consists of 2–3 single notes followed by a trill, often paraphrased as *dick dick dick-cissel;* flight call is a buzzerlike *bzrrrrt.*
Status: abundant summer resident.
Habitat: weedy fields and meadows, croplands and grasslands; grassy roadsides.

Similar Birds

Eastern Meadowlark

Western Meadowlark
(p. 214)

American Goldfinch
(p. 226)

streaked gray head

white chin and black "bib"

gray nape

yellow eyebrow

♂

♀

yellow breast with gray sides

Nesting: on or near the ground; well concealed among tall, dense vegetation; female builds a bulky, open cup nest of grass and other vegetation; pale blue eggs are ⅞ x ⅝ in; female incubates 4 eggs for 11–13 days.

Did You Know?

Dickcissels are polygynous, and males may mate with up to eight females in a single breeding season.

Look For

Breeding males perch atop tall blades of grass, fence posts and telephone wires, singing stuttering, trilled renditions of their own name throughout the day.

Red-winged Blackbird

Agelaius phoeniceus

The male Red-winged Blackbird wears his bright red shoulders like armor—together with his short, raspy song, they are key in defending his territory from rivals. In field experiments, males whose red shoulders were painted black soon lost their territories. • Nearly every cattail marsh and most roadside ditches in Kansas host Red-winged Blackbirds during at least some of the year. • The female looks like a huge streaky-breasted sparrow. Her cryptic coloration allows her to sit inconspicuously on her nest, blending in perfectly with the surroundings.

Other ID: *Male:* black overall. *Female:* mottled brown upperparts; pale "eyebrow."
Size: L 7½–9 in; W 13 in.
Voice: song is a loud, raspy *konk-a-ree* or *ogle-reeeee;* calls include a harsh check and high *tseert;* female gives a loud *che-che-che chee chee chee.*
Status: common migrant and summer resident; large flocks can be found in winter.
Habitat: cattail marshes, wet meadows and ditches, croplands and shoreline shrubs.

Similar Birds

Brewer's Blackbird

Rusty Blackbird

Brown-headed Cowbird (p. 218)

faint, red
shoulder patch

red shoulder
patch edged
in yellow

pale pinkish
throat

heavily streaked
underparts

♀

♂

Nesting: colonial; in cattails or shoreline
bushes; female builds an open cup nest of
dried cattail leaves lined with fine grass; darkly
marked, pale bluish green eggs are 1 x ¾ in;
female incubates 3–4 eggs for 10–12 days.

Did You Know?

Some scientists believe
that the Red-winged
Blackbird is the most
abundant bird species
in North America.

Look For

As early as mid-March, the
male Red-winged Blackbird
sings his *konk-a-ree* song and
spreads his shoulders to display
his bright red wing-patches to
rivals and potential mates.

Western Meadowlark
Sturnella neglecta

Distinguishing this bird from its eastern twin might be one of the more challenging identification tests of Kansas birding. Where their ranges overlap, Western Meadowlarks prefer drier, shorter and more barren grasslands, whereas Easterns prefer wetter areas and taller vegetation. The different songs are the easiest and most accurate way to distinguish these species. • The Western Meadowlark is our state bird.

Other ID: *Breeding:* mottled brown upperparts; brown crown stripes and eye line border; pale eyebrow and median crown stripe; yellow on throat extends onto lower cheek; long, pinkish legs; short, wide tail with white outer tail feathers. *Nonbreeding:* paler plumage.
Size: *L* 9–9½ in; *W* 14½ in.
Voice: song is rich, melodic series of bubbly, flutelike notes; calls include a low, loud *chuck* or *chup,* a rattling flight call or a few clear whistled notes.
Status: common year-round resident and migrant in western two-thirds of Kansas; uncommon in eastern Kansas where Eastern Meadowlark occurs more frequently.
Habitat: grassy meadows, native prairie and pastures; croplands and weedy fields.

Similar Birds

Eastern Meadowlark

Dickcissel
(p. 210)

Bobolink

yellow lores

long, sharp bill

dark streaking on white sides and flanks

broad, black breast band

yellow underparts

breeding

Nesting: in a depression or scrape on the ground in dense grass; domed grass nest with side entrance is woven into surrounding vegetation; brown- and purple-spotted, white eggs are 1⅛ x ⅞ in; female incubates 3–7 eggs for 13–15 days.

Did You Know?

Eastern Meadowlarks and Western Meadowlarks may occasionally interbreed, but their offspring are infertile.

Look For

Watch for the Western Meadowlark's courtship dance. Potential partners face each other, raise their bills high in the air and perform a grassland ballet.

Common Grackle
Quiscalus quiscula

The Common Grackle is a poor but spirited singer. Usually while perched in a shrub, a male grackle will take a deep breath to inflate his breast, then close his eyes and give out a loud, strained *tssh-schleek*. He remains smug despite his lack of musical talent, posing with his bill held high. • In fall, large flocks of Common Grackles are found in rural areas. Smaller bands occasionally venture into urban neighborhoods, where they assert their dominance at backyard bird feeders.

Other ID: long keeled tail. *Female:* smaller, duller and browner than male. *Juvenile:* dull brown overall; dark eyes.
Size: *L* 11–13½ in; *W* 17 in.
Voice: song is a series of harsh, strained notes ending with a metallic squeak: *tssh-schleek* or *gri-de-leeek*; call is a quick, loud *swaaaack* or *chaack*.
Status: common migrant and summer resident; rare winter resident.
Habitat: wetlands, hedgerows, fields, riparian woodlands; also shrubby parks and gardens.

Similar Birds

Rusty Blackbird

Brewer's Blackbird

Great-tailed Grackle

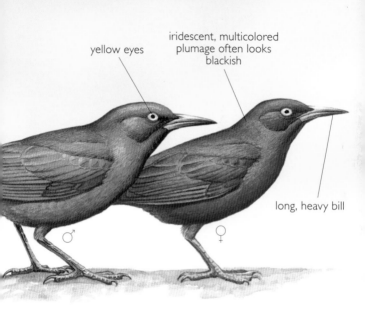

yellow eyes

iridescent, multicolored plumage often looks blackish

long, heavy bill

♂   ♀

Nesting: singly or in a small colony; in dense tree, shrub or emergent vegetation; often near water; female builds a bulky, open cup nest of twigs, grass, plant fibers and mud and lines it with fine grass or feathers; brown-blotched, pale blue eggs are 1⅛ x ⅞ in; female incubates 4–5 eggs for 12–14 days.

Did You Know?

At night, grackles commonly roost with groups of European Starlings, Red-winged Blackbirds and even Brown-headed Cowbirds.

Look For

Compared to other blackbirds the Common Grackle has a long, wedge-shaped tail that trails behind in flight.

Brown-headed Cowbird
Molothrus ater

These nomads historically followed bison herds across the Great Plains (they now follow cattle), so they never stayed in one area long enough to build and tend a nest. Instead, cowbirds lay their eggs in other birds' nests, relying on the unsuspecting adoptive parents to incubate the eggs and feed the aggressive young. Orioles, warblers, vireos and tanagers are among the most affected species. Increased livestock farming and fragmentation of forests has encouraged the expansion of the cowbird's range. It is known to parasitize more than 140 bird species.

Other ID: dark eyes; thick, conical bill.
Size: *L* 6–8 in; *W* 12 in.
Voice: song is a high, liquidy gurgle: *glug-ahl-whee* or *bubbloozeee;* call is a squeaky, high-pitched *seep, psee* or *wee-tse-tse* or fast, chipping *ch-ch-ch-ch-ch-ch.*
Status: common migrant and summer resident; uncommon winter resident.
Habitat: agricultural and residential areas, woodland edges, roadsides, landfills and areas near cattle.

Similar Birds

Rusty Blackbird

Brewer's Blackbird

Yellow-headed Blackbird

pale throat

dark brown head

light brown underparts with faint streaking ♀

♂

iridescent, green-blue plumage looks glossy black

Nesting: does not build a nest; female lays up to 30 eggs a year in the nests of other birds, usually 1 egg per nest; brown-speckled, whitish eggs are ⅞ x ⅝ in; eggs hatch after 10–13 days.

Did You Know?

When courting a female, the male cowbird points his bill upward to the sky, fans his tail and wings and utters a loud *squeek*.

Look For

When cowbirds feed in flocks, they hold their back ends up high, with their tails sticking straight up in the air.

Baltimore Oriole
Icterus galbula

With a flutelike song and a preference for the cano-
pies of neighborhood trees, the Baltimore Oriole is
difficult to spot, and a hanging pouch nest dangling
in a bare tree in autumn is sometimes the only evidence that the bird was there at all. • The planting
of trees around farms and in towns has allowed the
Baltimore Oriole to expand westward across the
formerly treeless plains. In extreme western Kansas,
Baltimore Orioles are replaced by Bullock's Orioles.
Until recently they were considered one species, and
hybrids can be found in western Kansas.

Other ID: *Female:* olive brown upperparts, darkest on
head; white wing bar.
Size: *L* 7–8 in; *W* 11½ in.
Voice: song consists of slow, clear whistles: *peter
peter peter here peter;* calls include a 2-note *tea-too*
and a rapid chatter: *ch-ch-ch-ch-ch.*
Status: common migrant and summer resident,
except in extreme western Kansas
where it is a rare breeding species.
Habitat: deciduous and mixed forests, particularly riparian woodlands;
natural openings, shorelines, roadsides,
orchards, gardens and parklands.

Similar Birds

Orchard Oriole

Bullock's Oriole

Black-headed
Grosbeak

black hood, back, wings and central tail feathers

white wing patch and feather edgings

♀

♂

dull yellow-orange under-parts and rump

bright orange under-parts, shoulder, rump and outer tail feathers

Nesting: high in a deciduous tree; female builds a hanging pouch nest of grass, bark shreds and grapevines; darkly marked, pale gray to bluish white eggs are ⅞ x ⅝ in; female incubates 4–5 eggs for 12–14 days.

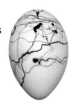

Did You Know?

Orioles spend more than half of each year in the tropics of Central and South America.

Look For

Baltimore Orioles are regular visitors to backyard feeders, especially if orange halves or grape jelly are offered.

House Finch
Carpodacus mexicanus

A native to western North America, the House Finch was brought to eastern parts of the continent as an illegally captured cage bird known as the "Hollywood Finch." In the early 1940s, New York pet shop owners released their birds to avoid prosecution and fines, and it is likely the descendants of those birds that colonized the eastern U.S. Meanwhile, House Finches were also expanding into Kansas from the west. The House Finch is now commonly found throughout the continental U.S. and has been introduced in Hawaii. • Only the House Finch has been aggressive enough to outcompete the House Sparrow. Both birds flourish in urban environments.

Other ID: streaked undertail coverts. *Female:* indistinct facial patterning; heavily streaked underparts.
Size: L 5–6 in; W 9½ in.
Voice: song is a bright, disjointed warble lasting about 3 seconds, often ending with a harsh *jeeer* or *wheer;* flight call is a sweet *cheer,* given singly or in a series.
Status: common year-round resident.
Habitat: cities, towns and agricultural areas.

Similar Birds

Purple Finch   Red Crossbill   Common Redpoll

short, conical bill

brown-streaked back

bright red eyebrow, forecrown, throat and breast

♂

♀

heavily streaked flanks

square tail

Nesting: in a cavity, building, dense foliage or abandoned bird nest; open cup nest of plants and other debris; pale blue, spotted eggs are ¾ x ⁹⁄₁₆ in; female incubates 4–5 eggs for 12–14 days.

Did You Know?

The male House Finch's plumage varies in color from light yellow to bright red, but females will choose the reddest males with which to breed.

Look For

In flight, the House Finch has a square tail, while the similar-looking Purple Finch has a sharply notched tail.

Pine Siskin
Carduelis pinus

Pine Siskins are unpredictable, social birds that may be abundant for a time, then suddenly disappear. Since their favored habitats are widely scattered, flocks are constantly on the move, searching forests for the most lucrative seed crops. • These drab, sparrowlike birds are easy to overlook at first, but once you recognize their characteristic rising *zzz-reeeee* calls and boisterous chatter, you will encounter them with surprising frequency. They often feed near the treetops, favoring coniferous and mixed woodlands and forest edges. They also visit bird feeders, especially thistle feeders.

Other ID: dull wing bars; indistinct facial pattern. *In flight:* yellow highlights at base of tail feathers and on wings.
Size: *L* 4½–5½ in; *W* 9 in.
Voice: song is a variable, bubbly mix of squeaky, raspy, metallic notes, sometimes resembling a jerky laugh; call is a buzzy, rising *zzzreeeee*.
Status: highly variable, but in some years it is a common migrant and winter resident; rare breeding species.
Habitat: woodlands and cemetaries, especially if pines are present; forest edges, roadsides, agricultural fields and backyards with feeders.

Similar Birds

Common Redpoll

Purple Finch, female

House Finch, female
(p. 222)

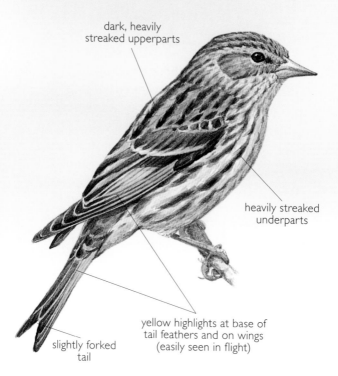

dark, heavily
streaked upperparts

heavily streaked
underparts

yellow highlights at base of
tail feathers and on wings
(easily seen in flight)

slightly forked
tail

Nesting: nests locally in Kansas and throughout
the western states and across Canada; usually
loosely colonial; typically on an outer branch of
a conifer; female builds a loose cup nest of twigs
and grass, and lines it with finer material; darkly
spotted, pale blue eggs are ⅝ x ½ in; female
incubates 3–5 eggs for about 13 days.

Did You Know?

The best way to meet
these birds is to set up
a finch feeder filled with
black niger seed in your
backyard and wait for
them to appear.

Look For

Pine Siskins are attracted to
road salts, mineral licks and
ashes, all of which add miner-
als to their diet.

American Goldfinch
Carduelis tristis

With their distinctive undulating flight style, American Goldfinches are hard to miss as they cheerily flutter over weedy fields, gardens and along roadsides. • Because these acrobatic birds regularly feed while hanging upside down, finch feeders are designed with the seed-openings below the perches. These feeders discourage the more aggressive House Sparrows, which feed upright, from stealing the seeds. Use niger or black-oil sunflower seeds to attract American Goldfinches to your bird feeder. • This species is often mistakenly called "Wild Canary."

Other ID: *Female:* yellow throat and breast; yellow-green belly. *Nonbreeding male:* olive brown back; yellow-tinged head; gray underparts.
Size: L 4½–5 in; W 9 in.
Voice: song is a long, varied series of trills, twitters, warbles and hissing notes; calls include *po-ta-to-chip* or *per-chic-or-ee* (often delivered in flight) and a whistled *dear-me, see-me*.
Status: common year-round resident, increasing in winter with northern birds joining local birds.
Habitat: weedy fields, woodland edges, meadows, riparian areas, parks and gardens.

Similar Birds

Evening Grosbeak

Lesser Goldfinch

yellow-green
upperparts

black wings
with white
wing bars

black cap
extends onto
forehead

♀

orange bill

♂

white rump
and undertail
coverts

orange legs

breeding

Nesting: in a fork of a deciduous tree; compact
cup nest is made of plant fibers, grass and spider
silk; pale bluish, spotted eggs are ⅝ x ½ in;
female incubates 4–6 eggs for 12–14 days.

Did You Know?

These birds nest in late
summer to ensure that
there is a dependable
source of seeds from
thistles and dandelions to
feed their young.

Look For

American Goldfinches delight
in perching on late-summer
thistle heads or poking
through dandelion patches
in search of seeds.

House Sparrow
Passer domesticus

The House Sparrow is not a true sparrow, but is an Old World weaver finch. This adaptive, aggressive species' tendency to usurp territory has led to local declines in native bird populations. • This abundant, conspicuous bird was introduced to North America in the 1850s as part of a plan to control insects that were damaging grain and cereal crops. As it turns out, the House Sparrow is largely vegetarian! • Although still abundant, its population may now be decreasing across North America.

Other ID: *Breeding male:* gray crown; black bill; dark, mottled upperparts; gray underparts; white wing bar. *Female:* indistinct facial pattern; plain gray-brown overall; streaked upperparts. *Nonbreeding male:* smaller black "bib"; pale bill.
Size: L 5½–6½ in; W 9½ in.
Voice: song is a plain, familiar *cheep-cheep-cheep-cheep*; call is a short *chill-up*.
Status: abundant year-round resident.
Habitat: urban and suburban areas, farmyards and agricultural areas, railroad yards and other developed areas.

Similar Birds

Harris's Sparrow
(p. 196)

Look For

In spring, House Sparrows feast on the buds of fruit trees and will sometimes eat lettuce from your backyard garden.

buffy eyebrow

chestnut nape

black lore and "bib"

♀

light gray cheek

♂

breeding

Nesting: often communal; in a human-made structure, ornamental shrub or natural cavity; pair builds a large dome nest of grass, twigs and plant fibers; gray-speckled, white to greenish eggs are ⅞ x ⅝ in; pair incubates 4–6 eggs for 10–13 days.

Did You Know?

House Sparrows have a high reproductive output. A pair may raise up to four clutches per year, with up to eight young per clutch.

Glossary

brood: *n.* a family of young from one hatching; *v.* to sit on eggs so as to hatch them.

buteo: a high-soaring hawk (genus *Buteo*); characterized by broad wings and a short, wide tail; feeds mostly on small mammals and other land animals.

cere: a fleshy area at the base of a bird's bill that contains the nostrils.

clutch: the number of eggs laid by the female at one time.

corvid: a member of the crow family (Corvidae); includes crows, jays, ravens and magpies.

covey: a group of birds, usually grouse or quail.

crop: an enlargement of the esophagus; serves as a storage structure and (in pigeons) has glands that produce secretions.

cryptic: a coloration pattern that helps to conceal the bird.

dabbling: a foraging technique used by ducks, in which the head and neck are submerged but the body and tail remain on the water's surface; dabbling ducks can usually walk easily on land, can take off without running and have brightly colored speculums.

endangered: facing imminent extirpation or extinction.

fledgling: a young bird that has left the nest but is dependent upon its parents.

flushing: a behavior in which frightened birds explode into flight in response to a disturbance.

flycatching: a feeding behavior in which the bird leaves a perch, snatches an insect in midair and returns to the same perch.

hawking: attempting to catch insects through aerial pursuit.

leading edge: the front edge of the wing as viewed from below.

mantle: feathers of the back and upperside of folded wings.

morph: one of several alternate plumages displayed by members of a species.

nocturnal: active during the night.

primaries: the outermost flight feathers.

raptor: a carnivorous (meat-eating) bird; includes eagles, hawks, falcons and owls.

riparian: refers to habitat along riverbanks.

rufous: rusty red in color.

special concern: a species that has characteristics that make it particularly sensitive to human activities or disturbance, requires a very specific or unique habitat or whose status is such that it requires careful monitoring.

speculum: a brightly colored patch on the wings of many dabbling ducks.

stoop: a steep dive through the air, usually performed by birds of prey while foraging or during courtship displays.

threatened: likely to become endangered in the near future in all or part of its range.

Checklist

The following checklist contains 469 species of birds that have been officially recorded in Kansas. Species are grouped by family and listed in taxonomic order in accordance with the A.O.U. *Check-list of North American Birds* (7th ed.) and its supplements.

Accidental and casual species (those that are not seen on a yearly basis) are listed in *italics*. In addition, the following risk categories are also noted: extinct or extirpated (ex), endangered (en) and threatened (th).

We wish to thank the Kansas Ornithological Society for providing the information for this checklist.

Waterfowl
- ❏ Black-bellied Whistling-Duck
- ❏ Fulvous Whistling-Duck
- ❏ Greater White-fronted Goose
- ❏ Snow Goose
- ❏ Ross's Goose
- ❏ Brant
- ❏ Cackling Goose
- ❏ Canada Goose
- ❏ Trumpeter Swan
- ❏ Tundra Swan
- ❏ Wood Duck
- ❏ Gadwall
- ❏ *Eurasian Wigeon*
- ❏ American Wigeon
- ❏ American Black Duck
- ❏ Mallard
- ❏ Mottled Duck
- ❏ Blue-winged Teal
- ❏ Cinnamon Teal
- ❏ Northern Shoveler
- ❏ Northern Pintail
- ❏ *Garganey*
- ❏ Green-winged Teal
- ❏ Canvasback
- ❏ Redhead
- ❏ Ring-necked Duck
- ❏ *Tufted Duck*
- ❏ Greater Scaup
- ❏ Lesser Scaup
- ❏ *King Eider*
- ❏ *Common Eider*
- ❏ *Harlequin Duck*
- ❏ Surf Scoter
- ❏ White-winged Scoter
- ❏ Black Scoter
- ❏ Long-tailed Duck
- ❏ Bufflehead
- ❏ Common Goldeneye
- ❏ Barrow's Goldeneye
- ❏ Hooded Merganser
- ❏ Common Merganser
- ❏ Red-breasted Merganser
- ❏ Ruddy Duck

Grouse & Allies
- ❏ Ring-necked Pheasant
- ❏ Ruffed Grouse
- ❏ Gunnison Sage-Grouse (ex)
- ❏ Sharp-tailed Grouse
- ❏ Greater Prairie-Chicken
- ❏ Lesser Prairie-Chicken
- ❏ Wild Turkey

New World Quail
- ❏ Scaled Quail
- ❏ Northern Bobwhite

Loons
- ❏ Red-throated Loon
- ❏ Pacific Loon
- ❏ Common Loon
- ❏ *Yellow-billed Loon*

Grebes
- ❏ Pied-billed Grebe
- ❏ Horned Grebe
- ❏ Red-necked Grebe

☐ Eared Grebe
☐ Western Grebe
☐ Clark's Grebe

Pelicans
☐ American White Pelican
☐ Brown Pelican

Cormorants
☐ Neotropic Cormorant
☐ Double-crested Cormorant

Darters
☐ Anhinga

Frigatebirds
☐ *Magnificent Frigatebird*

Herons
☐ American Bittern
☐ Least Bittern
☐ Great Blue Heron
☐ Great Egret
☐ Snowy Egret
☐ Little Blue Heron
☐ Tricolored Heron
☐ *Reddish Egret*
☐ Cattle Egret
☐ Green Heron
☐ Black-crowned Night-Heron
☐ Yellow-crowned Night-Heron

Ibises & Spoonbills
☐ White Ibis
☐ Glossy Ibis
☐ White-faced Ibis
☐ *Roseate Spoonbill*

Storks
☐ Wood Stork

Vultures
☐ Black Vulture
☐ Turkey Vulture

Flamingos
☐ *Greater Flamingo*

Kites, Hawks & Eagles
☐ Osprey
☐ Swallow-tailed Kite
☐ *White-tailed Kite*
☐ Mississippi Kite
☐ Bald Eagle (th)
☐ Northern Harrier
☐ Sharp-shinned Hawk
☐ Cooper's Hawk
☐ Northern Goshawk

☐ *Harris's Hawk*
☐ Red-shouldered Hawk
☐ Broad-winged Hawk
☐ *Gray Hawk*
☐ Swainson's Hawk
☐ Red-tailed Hawk
☐ Ferruginous Hawk
☐ Rough-legged Hawk
☐ Golden Eagle

Falcons
☐ American Kestrel
☐ Merlin
☐ *Gyrfalcon*
☐ Peregrine Falcon (en)
☐ Prairie Falcon

Rails, Gallinules & Coots
☐ Yellow Rail
☐ Black Rail
☐ King Rail
☐ Virginia Rail
☐ Sora
☐ Purple Gallinule
☐ Common Moorhen
☐ American Coot

Cranes
☐ Sandhill Crane
☐ Whooping Crane (en)

Plovers
☐ Black-bellied Plover
☐ American Golden-Plover
☐ Snowy Plover (th)
☐ *Wilson's Plover*
☐ Semipalmated Plover
☐ Piping Plover (th)
☐ Killdeer
☐ Mountain Plover

Stilts & Avocets
☐ Black-Necked Stilt
☐ American Avocet

Sandpipers & Allies
☐ Spotted Sandpiper
☐ Solitary Sandpiper
☐ *Spotted Redshank*
☐ Greater Yellowlegs
☐ Willet
☐ Lesser Yellowlegs
☐ Upland Sandpiper
☐ Eskimo Curlew (en)
☐ Whimbrel
☐ Long-billed Curlew

- ❏ Hudsonian Godwit
- ❏ Marbled Godwit
- ❏ Ruddy Turnstone
- ❏ Red Knot
- ❏ Sanderling
- ❏ Semipalmated Sandpiper
- ❏ Western Sandpiper
- ❏ Least Sandpiper
- ❏ White-rumped Sandpiper
- ❏ Baird's Sandpiper
- ❏ Pectoral Sandpiper
- ❏ Dunlin
- ❏ *Curlew Sandpiper*
- ❏ Stilt Sandpiper
- ❏ Buff-breasted Sandpiper
- ❏ *Ruff*
- ❏ Short-billed Dowitcher
- ❏ Long-billed Dowitcher
- ❏ Wilson's Snipe
- ❏ American Woodcock
- ❏ Wilson's Phalarope
- ❏ Red-necked Phalarope
- ❏ Red Phalarope

Gulls & Allies
- ❏ Laughing Gull
- ❏ Franklin's Gull
- ❏ Little Gull
- ❏ *Black-headed Gull*
- ❏ Bonaparte's Gull
- ❏ *Mew Gull*
- ❏ Ring-billed Gull
- ❏ California Gull
- ❏ Herring Gull
- ❏ Thayer's Gull
- ❏ *Iceland Gull*
- ❏ Lesser Black-backed Gull
- ❏ *Glaucous-winged Gull*
- ❏ Glaucous Gull
- ❏ Great Black-backed Gull
- ❏ Sabine's Gull
- ❏ Black-legged Kittiwake
- ❏ Least Tern (en)
- ❏ *Gull-billed Tern*
- ❏ Caspian Tern
- ❏ Black Tern
- ❏ Common Tern
- ❏ *Arctic Tern*
- ❏ Forster's Tern
- ❏ *Black Skimmer*

Jaegers
- ❏ *Pomarine Jaeger*
- ❏ Parasitic Jaeger

- ❏ *Long-tailed Jaeger*

Murrelets
- ❏ *Long-billed Murrelet*

Pigeons & Doves
- ❏ Rock Pigeon
- ❏ *Band-tailed Pigeon*
- ❏ Eurasian Collared-Dove
- ❏ White-winged Dove
- ❏ Mourning Dove
- ❏ Passenger Pigeon (ex)
- ❏ Inca Dove
- ❏ Common Ground-Dove

Parakeets
- ❏ Carolina Parakeet (ex)

Cuckoos, Roadrunners & Anis
- ❏ Yellow-billed Cuckoo
- ❏ Black-billed Cuckoo
- ❏ Greater Roadrunner
- ❏ Groove-billed Ani

Barn Owls
- ❏ Barn Owl

Owls
- ❏ *Flammulated Owl*
- ❏ Western Screech-Owl
- ❏ Eastern Screech-Owl
- ❏ Great Horned Owl
- ❏ Snowy Owl
- ❏ Burrowing Owl
- ❏ Barred Owl
- ❏ Long-eared Owl
- ❏ Short-eared Owl
- ❏ Northern Saw-whet Owl

Nightjars
- ❏ *Lesser Nighthawk*
- ❏ Common Nighthawk
- ❏ Common Poor-will
- ❏ Chuck-will's-widow
- ❏ Whip-poor-will

Swifts
- ❏ Chimney Swift
- ❏ *White-throated Swift*

Hummingbirds
- ❏ *Broad-billed Hummingbird*
- ❏ *Magnificent Hummingbird*
- ❏ Ruby-throated Hummingbird
- ❏ Black-chinned Hummingbird
- ❏ *Anna's Hummingbird*
- ❏ *Costa's Hummingbird*

- ❏ Calliope Hummingbird
- ❏ Broad-tailed Hummingbird
- ❏ Rufous Hummingbird
- ❏ *Allen's Hummingbird*

Kingfishers
- ❏ Belted Kingfisher

Woodpeckers
- ❏ Lewis's Woodpecker
- ❏ Red-headed Woodpecker
- ❏ Red-bellied Woodpecker
- ❏ *Williamson's Sapsucker*
- ❏ Yellow-bellied Sapsucker
- ❏ *Red-naped Sapsucker*
- ❏ Ladder-backed Woodpecker
- ❏ Downy Woodpecker
- ❏ Hairy Woodpecker
- ❏ *American Three-toed Woodpecker*
- ❏ Northern Flicker
- ❏ Pileated Woodpecker

Flycatchers
- ❏ Olive-sided Flycatcher
- ❏ Western Wood-Pewee
- ❏ Eastern Wood-Pewee
- ❏ Yellow-bellied Flycatcher
- ❏ Acadian Flycatcher
- ❏ Alder Flycatcher
- ❏ Willow Flycatcher
- ❏ Least Flycatcher
- ❏ *Hammond's Flycatcher*
- ❏ Gray Flycatcher
- ❏ Dusky Flycatcher
- ❏ *Cordilleran Flycatcher*
- ❏ Black Phoebe
- ❏ Eastern Phoebe
- ❏ Say's Phoebe
- ❏ Vermilion Flycatcher
- ❏ Ash-throated Flycatcher
- ❏ Great Crested Flycatcher
- ❏ *Great Kiskadee*
- ❏ Cassin's Kingbird
- ❏ Western Kingbird
- ❏ Eastern Kingbird
- ❏ Scissor-tailed Flycatcher
- ❏ *Fork-tailed Flycatcher*

Shrikes
- ❏ Loggerhead Shrike
- ❏ Northern Shrike

Vireos
- ❏ White-eyed Vireo
- ❏ Bell's Vireo
- ❏ *Black-capped Vireo* (en)
- ❏ *Gray Vireo*
- ❏ Yellow-throated Vireo
- ❏ *Plumbeous Vireo*
- ❏ *Cassin's Vireo*
- ❏ Blue-headed Vireo
- ❏ Warbling Vireo
- ❏ Philadelphia Vireo
- ❏ Red-eyed Vireo

Jays & Crows
- ❏ Steller's Jay
- ❏ Blue Jay
- ❏ Western Scrub-Jay
- ❏ *Mexican Jay*
- ❏ Pinyon Jay
- ❏ Clark's Nutcracker
- ❏ Black-billed Magpie
- ❏ American Crow
- ❏ Fish Crow
- ❏ Chihuahuan Raven
- ❏ Common Raven

Larks
- ❏ Horned Lark

Swallows
- ❏ Purple Martin
- ❏ Tree Swallow
- ❏ Violet-green Swallow
- ❏ Northern Rough-winged Swallow
- ❏ Bank Swallow
- ❏ Cliff Swallow
- ❏ *Cave Swallow*
- ❏ Barn Swallow

Chickadees & Titmice
- ❏ Carolina Chickadee
- ❏ Black-capped Chickadee
- ❏ Mountain Chickadee
- ❏ *Juniper Titmouse*
- ❏ Tufted Titmouse

Bushtits
- ❏ Bushtit

Nuthatches
- ❏ Red-breasted Nuthatch
- ❏ White-breasted Nuthatch
- ❏ *Pygmy Nuthatch*
- ❏ *Brown-headed Nuthatch*

Creepers
- ❏ Brown Creeper

Wrens
❏ Rock Wren
❏ *Canyon Wren*
❏ Carolina Wren
❏ Bewick's Wren
❏ House Wren
❏ Winter Wren
❏ Sedge Wren
❏ Marsh Wren

Kinglets
❏ Golden-crowned Kinglet
❏ Ruby-crowned Kinglet

Gnatcatchers
❏ Blue-gray Gnatcatcher

Thrushes
❏ *Northern Wheatear*
❏ Eastern Bluebird
❏ *Western Bluebird*
❏ Mountain Bluebird
❏ Townsend's Solitaire
❏ Veery
❏ Gray-cheeked Thrush
❏ Swainson's Thrush
❏ Hermit Thrush
❏ Wood Thrush
❏ American Robin
❏ Varied Thrush

Mockingbirds & Thrashers
❏ Gray Catbird
❏ Northern Mockingbird
❏ Sage Thrasher
❏ Brown Thrasher
❏ Curve-billed Thrasher

Starlings
❏ European Starling

Pipits
❏ American Pipit
❏ Sprague's Pipit

Waxwings
❏ Bohemian Waxwing
❏ Cedar Waxwing

Silky-flycatchers
❏ *Phainopepla*

Wood-warblers
❏ Blue-winged Warbler
❏ Golden-winged Warbler
❏ Tennessee Warbler
❏ Orange-crowned Warbler
❏ Nashville Warbler

❏ Virginia's Warbler
❏ Northern Parula
❏ Yellow Warbler
❏ Chestnut-sided Warbler
❏ Magnolia Warbler
❏ Cape May Warbler
❏ Black-throated Blue Warbler
❏ Yellow-rumped Warbler
❏ Black-throated Gray Warbler
❏ Black-throated Green Warbler
❏ Townsend's Warbler
❏ *Hermit Warbler*
❏ Blackburnian Warbler
❏ Yellow-throated Warbler
❏ Pine Warbler
❏ Prairie Warbler
❏ Palm Warbler
❏ Bay-breasted Warbler
❏ Blackpoll Warbler
❏ Cerulean Warbler
❏ Black-and-white Warbler
❏ American Redstart
❏ Prothonotary Warbler
❏ Worm-eating Warbler
❏ *Swainson's Warbler*
❏ Ovenbird
❏ Northern Waterthrush
❏ Louisiana Waterthrush
❏ Kentucky Warbler
❏ Connecticut Warbler
❏ Mourning Warbler
❏ MacGillivray's Warbler
❏ Common Yellowthroat
❏ Hooded Warbler
❏ Wilson's Warbler
❏ Canada Warbler
❏ *Painted Redstart*
❏ Yellow-breasted Chat

Tanagers
❏ *Hepatic Tanager*
❏ Summer Tanager
❏ Scarlet Tanager
❏ Western Tanager

Sparrows & Allies
❏ Green-tailed Towhee
❏ Spotted Towhee
❏ Eastern Towhee
❏ Canyon Towhee
❏ Cassin's Sparrow
❏ *Bachman's Sparrow*
❏ Rufous-crowned Sparrow
❏ American Tree Sparrow

- ❏ Chipping Sparrow
- ❏ Clay-colored Sparrow
- ❏ Brewer's Sparrow
- ❏ Field Sparrow
- ❏ Vesper Sparrow
- ❏ Lark Sparrow
- ❏ *Black-throated Sparrow*
- ❏ *Sage Sparrow*
- ❏ Lark Bunting
- ❏ Savannah Sparrow
- ❏ Grasshopper Sparrow
- ❏ Baird's Sparrow
- ❏ Henslow's Sparrow
- ❏ Le Conte's Sparrow
- ❏ Nelson's Sharp-tailed Sparrow
- ❏ Fox Sparrow
- ❏ Song Sparrow
- ❏ Lincoln's Sparrow
- ❏ Swamp Sparrow
- ❏ White-throated Sparrow
- ❏ Harris's Sparrow
- ❏ White-crowned Sparrow
- ❏ Golden-crowned Sparrow
- ❏ Dark-eyed Junco
- ❏ McCown's Longspur
- ❏ Lapland Longspur
- ❏ Smith's Longspur
- ❏ Chestnut-collared Longspur
- ❏ Snow Bunting

Grosbeaks & Buntings
- ❏ Northern Cardinal
- ❏ *Pyrrhuloxia*
- ❏ Rose-breasted Grosbeak
- ❏ Black-headed Grosbeak
- ❏ Blue Grosbeak

- ❏ Lazuli Bunting
- ❏ Indigo Bunting
- ❏ Painted Bunting
- ❏ Dickcissel

Blackbirds & Allies
- ❏ Bobolink
- ❏ Red-winged Blackbird
- ❏ Eastern Meadowlark
- ❏ Western Meadowlark
- ❏ Yellow-headed Blackbird
- ❏ Rusty Blackbird
- ❏ Brewer's Blackbird
- ❏ Common Grackle
- ❏ Great-tailed Grackle
- ❏ Brown-headed Cowbird
- ❏ Orchard Oriole
- ❏ Bullock's Oriole
- ❏ Baltimore Oriole
- ❏ *Scott's Oriole*

Finches
- ❏ *Brambling*
- ❏ Pine Grosbeak
- ❏ Purple Finch
- ❏ Cassin's Finch
- ❏ House Finch
- ❏ Red Crossbill
- ❏ White-winged Crossbill
- ❏ Common Redpoll
- ❏ Pine Siskin
- ❏ Lesser Goldfinch
- ❏ American Goldfinch
- ❏ Evening Grosbeak

Old World Sparrows
- ❏ House Sparrow

Select References

Busby, W.H. and J.L. Zimmerman. 2001. *Kansas Breeding Bird Atlas.* University of Kansas Press, Lawrence, KS.

Thompson, M.C. and C. Ely. 1989. *Birds of Kansas.* Vol. 1. University of Kansas Press, Lawrence, KS.

Thompson, M.C. and C. Ely. 1992. *Birds of Kansas.* Vol. 2. University of Kansas Press, Lawrence, KS.

Index